The Letter to the Ephesians

The Letter to the Ephesians

W. CURTIS VAUGHAN

Convention Press

NASHVILLE TENNESSEE

Code Number: Church Study Course
This book is number 0228 in category 2, section
for Adults and Young People.
Library of Congress Catalog Card Number: 63-16387
Printed in the United States of America
410. AL 63 R.R.D.

To my wife MARIAN
and our children CURT

BECKY

and STEPHEN

About the Author

W. CURTIS VAUGHAN was born in Humboldt, Tennessee, on October 30, 1924, but at an early age moved with his family to Memphis. He received the A.B. degree from Union University in Jackson, Tennessee, and upon completion of his college work attended Southwestern Baptist Theological Seminary in Fort Worth, Texas. There he earned the B.D. and Th.D. degrees.

While in college and seminary Mr. Vaughan served as pastor of churches near Jackson, Tennessee; Joshua, Texas; and Weatherford, Texas. Since 1950 he has been teaching in the Department of New Testament at Southwestern and has served as interim pastor of churches in Texas, Oklahoma, and Kansas.

In 1961, while on sabbatical leave from the seminary, he studied at the University of Manchester, England, and the University of Edinburgh, Scotland.

Contents

Church Study Course

THE CHURCH STUDY COURSE began October 1, 1959. It is a merger of three courses previously promoted by the Sunday School Board —the Sunday School Training Course, the Graded Training Union Study Course, and the Church Music Training Course. On October 1, 1961, the Woman's Missionary Union principles and methods studies were added.

The course is fully graded. The system of awards provides a series of five diplomas of twenty books each for Adults or Young People, two diplomas of five books each for Intermediates, and two diplomas of five books each for Juniors. Book awards earned previously in the Sunday School Training Course, the Graded Training Union Study Course, and the Church Music Training Course may be transferred to the new course.

The course is comprehensive, with books grouped into twenty categories. The purpose of the course is to help Christians to grow in knowledge and conviction, to help them to grow toward maturity in Christian character and competence for service, to encourage them to participate worthily as workers in their churches, and to develop leaders for all phases of church life and work.

The Church Study Course is promoted by the Baptist Sunday School Board, 127 Ninth Avenue, North, Nashville, Tennessee, through its Sunday School, Training Union, Church Music, and Church Administration departments; by the Woman's Missionary Union, 600 North Twentieth Street, Birmingham, Alabama; and by the respective departments in the states affiliated with the Southern Baptist Convention. A description of the course and the system of awards may be found in the leaflet "Trained Workmen," which may be obtained without charge from any one of these departments.

A record of all awards earned should be maintained in each church. A person should be designated by the church to keep the files. Forms for such records may be ordered from any Baptist Book Store.

Requirements for Credit in Class or Home Study

IF CREDIT is desired for the study of this book in a class or by home study, the following requirements must be met:

I. In Classwork

1. The class must meet a minimum of seven and one-half clock hours. The required time does not include assembly periods. Ten class periods of forty-five minutes each are recommended. (If laboratory or clinical work is desired in specialized or technical courses, this requirement may be met by six clock hours of classwork and three clock hours of supervised laboratory or clinical work.)

2. A class member who attends all class sessions and completes the reading of the book within a week following the last class session will not be required to do any written work for credit.

3. A class member who is absent from one or more sessions must answer the questions (pp. 144–146) on all chapters he misses. In such a case, he must turn in his paper within a week, and he must certify that he has read the book.

4. The teacher should request an award for himself. A person who teaches a book in the section for Intermediates or Juniors (any category) or conducts an approved unit of instruction for Nursery, Beginner, or Primary children will be granted an award in category 11, Special Studies, which will count as an elective on his own diploma. He should specify in his request the name of the book taught, or the unit conducted for Nursery, Beginner, or Primary children.

5. The teacher should complete the "Request for Book Awards —Class Study" (Form 150) and forward it within two weeks after the completion of the class to the Church Study Course Awards Office, 127 Ninth Avenue, North, Nashville 3, Tennessee.

II. In Home Study

1. A person who does not attend any class session may receive credit by answering all questions for written work as indicated in the book (pp. 144–146). When a person turns in his paper on home study, he must certify that he has read the book.

2. Students may find profit in studying the text together, but individual papers are required. Carbon copies or duplicates in any form cannot be accepted.

3. Home study work papers may be graded by the pastor or a person designated by him, or they may be sent to the Church Study Course Awards Office for grading. The form entitled "Request for Book Awards—Home Study" (Form 151) must be used in requesting awards. It should be mailed to Church Study Course Awards Office, 127 Ninth Avenue, North, Nashville 3, Tennessee.

III. Credit for This Book

This book is number 0228 in category 2, section for Adults and Young People.

Introduction

THIS VOLUME is designed as a manual merely to *guide* in the study of the epistle to the Ephesians. It provides a simple outline around which a brief discussion of the text is given. This guidebook aims to help you, the reader, to follow the course of Paul's argument in the Scripture passage, to point out for you some of the main emphases of the epistle, and to stimulate your interest for further study.

This guidebook is designed for use with your open Bible—both in your individual study and during class periods. To realize the most from this study, you must constantly refer to the text of Ephesians. Unless otherwise indicated all Scripture quotations in the guide are from the King James Version. However, you will find the use of several translations very stimulating.

The use of this guide will lead you in analytical studies, each based on the passage indicated at the head of a chapter. You are urged to read the whole passage before you take it up piece by piece in depth study. When you have completed the study outlined in this guidebook, return to the Scripture passage and read the whole of it again, thus putting together all the ideas you have gained. This principle of going from the whole to the detailed study then back to the whole is important in all Bible study.

The author does not expect everyone to agree with his interpretations. Indeed, there are a number of significant concepts in Ephesians about which even our Baptist people disagree. The writer has earnestly and honestly sought to understand the mind of Paul, remembering that the interpreter's first responsibility is to ascertain the meaning of the text. To approach God's Word with a preconceived notion as to what it ought to say or to force it to say what one wants it to say is to do violence to the Scriptures.

It is not possible to mention all who have helped in the preparation of this work. The author is especially indebted to Dr. Ray Summers, under whose teaching his special interest in Ephesians was first awakened and from whose life and lectures he has drawn constant strength and inspiration.

Quotations from *American Standard Version* (1929), are used by permission of the International Council of Religious Education. Those from *The New Testament in Modern English,* © J. B. Phillips, 1958, are used with permission of The Macmillan Company.

CHAPTER 1

1

Introducing Ephesians

EPHESIANS IS CONSIDERED by many people to be the greatest of Paul's writings. Indeed, many pronounce it the supreme book of the New Testament. Of all the epistles of Paul, it was John Calvin's favorite. John Knox, on his deathbed, frequently had read to him from Calvin's sermons on the letter to the Ephesians. From this epistle John Bunyan received much of the inspiration for his allegory, *The Pilgrim's Progress*. Across the centuries Ephesians has been an inexhaustible source book for gospel preaching. In every generation it has nurtured the faith of our Baptist people, and its language forms the basis for many of our hymns.

I. THE CHARACTER OF THE LETTER

One man has called Ephesians "the most sublime, the most profound, the most advanced and final utterance of St. Paul's Gospel to the Gentiles." [1] With its emphasis on a reigning God whose purpose for the world must ultimately prevail, no book of the New Testament is more relevant to our day than this epistle.

1. *A Prison Letter*

Ephesians belongs to the prison literature of the Bible, for when it was composed the author was obviously in some kind of enforced confinement. He calls himself "the prisoner of Jesus Christ" (3:1), "the prisoner of the Lord" (4:1), "an ambassador in bonds" (6:20). Conservative scholars generally agree that the allusions are to the period of Paul's first

1

Roman imprisonment. This assumption would make the date of Ephesians somewhere in the neighborhood of A.D. 61–63.

2. A Comprehensive Letter

Ephesians is the most general of all of Paul's epistles. It has a wider outlook than any other epistle of the New Testament, with the possible exception of Romans. The sweep of its thought takes in Jew and Gentile, heaven and earth, past and present, and the ages yet to come.

This wide outlook in Ephesians is pointed up by the frequent occurrence of the word "all," found in it more than fifty times. For example, God is said to be working *all* things after the counsel of his will. He is over *all*, through *all*, and in *all*. He created *all* things, sums up *all* things in Christ, and is able to do exceeding abundantly above *all* that we ask or think. Christ sits far above *all* rule and authority and power and dominion and every name that is named. *All* things are put into subjection under his feet, and he fills *all* in *all*.

3. A Doctrinal Letter

Ephesians contains the last lengthy theological discussion which we have from the pen of Paul. All of it is especially marked by its profound thought. It has much to say about the mystery (the unveiled secret) of redemption and the divine intention for the human race. It treats such majestic themes as the grace of God, the sovereignty of God, the fulness of God, predestination, reconciliation, union with Christ, and the church as the body of Christ. In the words of one scholar, it is "the distilled essence of the Christian religion," and "the most authoritative and most consummate compendium of our holy Christian faith." [2]

4. A Practical Letter

For all its profound doctrine, Ephesians is an intensely practical letter. It comes to grips with moral, spiritual, and domestic problems and gives answers in clear language. Its ethical principles have abiding value and are such as to regulate the whole of life.

5. *A Devotional Letter*

In Ephesians, as in no other of his epistles, Paul seems to teach on his knees. This characteristic is particularly true of the first three chapters, where the great doctrinal discussion is cast in the form of a devotional meditation.

II. THE THEME OF THE LETTER

Many interpreters feel that the central theme of Ephesians is unity—particularly the unity of the church as the body of Christ. But this idea is simply a part of the larger concept of God's eternal purpose for unifying all things in Christ (Eph. 1:10). Accordingly, the letter to the Ephesians may be seen as Paul's *inspired exposition of God's purpose for the human race*.

But along with this emphasis on the divine purpose is another strand of thought in Ephesians which centers in the concept of *the people of God*. Throughout the Ephesian letter Paul insists that God is working out his great purpose for mankind by calling men to Christ and by forming in Christ a new redeemed society. This redeemed society, which constitutes God's new people, is referred to in various ways in the letter—for example as God's heritage, God's building, Christ's body, the church, one new man. The main idea in all these figures is that God now has an elect people in the world. Through them his purpose is being worked out and through them he plans to effect his intention for the whole universe.

III. SIMILARITY TO THE COLOSSIAN LETTER

Ephesians and Colossians are companion epistles. There are, to be sure, significant differences between them, but the likenesses are even more remarkable. They are alike, for instance, in historical background. Both epistles were written by Paul while he was a prisoner. Both were intended originally for believers in Asia. Both were entrusted to Tychicus, the messenger who was to bear them to their respective destinations (cf. Col. 4:7; Eph. 6:21). Apparently both letters were written at nearly the same time and were called forth by similar circumstances.

The salutations and the general structure of the two letters are similar, and many of the topics treated are common to both. Even the language is remarkably similar. It has been estimated that of the 155 verses of Ephesians over half contain expressions identical with those in Colossians. Ephesians seems to be an expansion by Paul of ideas presented in compact form in Colossians. That epistle—terse, abrupt, argumentative—is the sketch of which Ephesians—calm, meditative, instructive—is the finished picture.

IV. OPENING THE LETTER (1:1-2)

The first two verses of Ephesians make up the salutation. (Now would be a good time to read them if you have not already done so.) This type of salutation was the usual way of starting a letter in Paul's day. The custom was to give first the name of the writer, then to identify the reader or readers, and finally to express greeting. Paul in his letters followed this pattern. However, he always gave it a decidedly Christian flavor and varied and amplified it according to circumstances.

1. *The Writer* (v. 1a)

This epistle, like twelve other New Testament books, begins with the name "Paul." Saul was his Jewish name; Paul was his Roman name. Very likely he had both names from his birth, but as his Christian witnessing took him more and more into contact with the Roman world he began to use the name that would identify him as having a part in that world.

Paul makes two assertions about himself in these opening words. First, he affirms that he is "an apostle of Christ Jesus." The term "apostle" literally means "a person sent, a messenger." It is found more than eighty times in the New Testament, mostly in the writings of Paul and Luke.

In non-Christian literature the word was sometimes used of a naval squadron sent out on an expedition, or of an ambassador sent out by a government. In the New Testament the word "apostle" regularly denotes a person engaged by another to carry out a commission. The word is used of Jesus as the Sent One of God (Heb. 3:1), of those sent out to preach to Israel (Luke 11:49), and of messengers sent out by the churches (2 Cor. 8:23; Phil. 2:25). But the principal use of "apostle" in the New Testament is in reference to that select group of men who had a special and direct commission from Christ and who went forth endued with his power and clothed with his authority. In affirming his apostleship, therefore, Paul is actually asserting his right to address his readers, and in essence is declaring that the teaching which he sets forth is invested with divine authority.

Paul further declares that his apostleship is "through the will of God" (thus strengthening the concept of authority). This phrase emphasizes the divine origin of his apostleship and thus shows the source of Paul's authority. Apostleship was not something which he had arrogantly taken to himself; his entrance on the office was "not of men" (Gal. 1:1) but was an act of sovereign grace. (Cf. 1 Cor. 1:1; 2 Cor. 1:1; 2 Tim. 1:1.) Paul's tone is not that of pride but rather of sheer amazement.

2. The Readers (v. 1b)

The readers to whom the epistle was first sent are addressed as "the saints which are at Ephesus, and . . . the faithful in Christ Jesus." Observe first that they are "saints."

The New Testament uses several names for the people of God in the apostolic period—"believers," "disciples," "followers of the way," "brethren," "Christians." But one of the most characteristic designations is "saint." The root meaning of the word is separation or consecration, the suggestion being that Christians are people whom God has set apart for himself. In the biblical use of the word all Christians are saints.

This epistle is addressed to the saints who lived "at Ephesus." The words "at Ephesus," though found in the great majority of the Greek manuscripts, do not occur in the three oldest and best manuscripts of this letter. Evidently, the letter was originally a circular epistle intended for all the churches of the Roman province of Asia (of which Ephesus was the capital city). When Paul wrote the letter he may have left a blank space so that each church, when making a copy of the original, could insert its own name. Ephesus was the chief city of the province, the center from which all of Asia was evangelized (Acts 19:10). The church at Ephesus likely first received this letter and later was entrusted with its safekeeping. Thus the letter eventually became identified exclusively with Ephesus.

This city was situated at the mouth of the Cayster River on the west coast of what is now Asiatic Turkey. Ephesus had from very early times been a city of considerable significance, but it was during the days of the Roman Empire that it reached the height of its importance. The city covered a vast area, and its population likely was more than a third of a million. It was the center of the worship of Diana, the goddess of fertility. The temple of Diana, located about a mile outside of Ephesus and considered one of the Seven Wonders of the ancient world, was the chief glory of the city.

A third description of the original readers of this letter is found in the words "faithful in Christ Jesus." This designation may mean they were faithful in the sense of being loyal to Christ Jesus. More likely it simply means they were believers in Christ. That is, they were people who had put their whole trust in Jesus as Son of God, Lord and Saviour. The expression "in Christ Jesus" suggests not only that he was the object of their faith but that they enjoyed a living union with him. Geographically they were at Ephesus, but spiritually they were in Christ Jesus.

3. *The Greeting* (v. 2)

Paul's greeting is in the form of a prayer. In it he wishes for his readers grace and peace from God. The usual Greek salutation was "Rejoice!" (*chairein*). Paul replaces this by the similar-sounding *charis* ("grace") and adds to it the usual Jewish greeting, "peace." Grace is God's free favor lavished upon the undeserving. "Peace" signified not simply the absence of strife but the presence of positive blessings. The word denotes wholeness, soundness, or prosperity, especially in spiritual things. It conveys essentially the idea of 3 John 2: "I pray that in all things thou mayest prosper and be in health, even as thy soul prospereth" (ASV).

NOTE: For suggestions for the study of this book, please read the Introduction on p. xi.

---

[1] F. W. Farrar, *The Messages of the Books* (New York: E. P. Dutton and Company, 1885), p. 328.

[2] John A. Mackay, *God's Order: The Ephesian Letter and this Present Time* (New York: The Macmillan Company, 1953), p. 15. Used with permission of the Macmillan Company.

CHAPTER 2

I. A Description of the Divine Blessings (1:3–6)
  1. Their Character (v. 3)
  2. The Sphere in Which They Are Experienced (v. 3)
  3. The Ground on Which They Come (vv. 4–6)
      (1) God's choice made in Christ (v. 4)
      (2) An eternal choice (v. 4)
      (3) A purposeful choice (vv. 4–5)
      (4) Unto himself (v. 5)
      (5) According to his will (v. 5)
      (6) To exhibit his grace (v. 6)

II. An Enumeration of the Divine Blessings (1:7–14)
  1. Redemption and Forgiveness (v. 7)
  2. Wisdom and Prudence (vv. 8–10)
  3. A Heavenly Heritage (vv. 11–12)
  4. The Gift of the Spirit (vv. 13–14)

2

The Blessings of God's New People:
A Doxology

Ephesians 1:3–14

MOST OF PAUL'S EPISTLES begin with an expression of thanks to God for certain spiritual qualities produced by divine grace and power in the readers' lives. Ephesians, however, is different. Here, instead of the customary thanksgiving, there is what may more appropriately be called a doxology, a majestic hymn of praise to God.

This outburst of adoring praise requires and rewards the closest study. Observe first its structure. In the Greek text verses 3–14 constitute one long, involved sentence. The King James Version, to help the reader keep the connection of thought, places a period at the end of verses 6, 12, and 14. Thus, this inspired hymn falls into three stanzas. The first (vv. 3–6) relates to the past and centers largely in the gracious purpose of the Father. The second (vv. 7–12) has to do with the present and revolves mainly around the redemptive work of Christ. The third (vv. 13–14) points to the future full accomplishment of redemption and magnifies the ministry of the Holy Spirit. Each stanza closes with a sort of refrain: "to the praise of the glory of his grace" (v. 6), "to the praise of his glory" (v. 12), and "unto the praise of his glory" (v. 14).

The entire passage may be seen as an ascription of praise to God for his gracious benefits to his people. The theme is struck in verse 3: "Blessed be the God . . . who hath blessed us with all spiritual blessings." Notice the joyous and emphatic reiteration: "blessed," "hath blessed," "blessings."

"Blessed" translates an adjective used in the New Testament always of God. The inference is that he alone has an unchanging claim on our homage. "Hath blessed" translates a verb, the tense of which sums up all the blessings of God and treats them as a single whole. The primary reference appears to be to those blessings that come to the believer in his experience of conversion, but the concept is broad enough to include every act of divine blessing.

Our blessing of God, it is implied, is in response to the blessings we have received from him. It is not, of course, that we add anything to him or bestow any benefit upon him. We bless God by acknowledging his mercy and offering praise and thanks to him for his goodness to us.

I. A Description of the Divine Blessings (1:3–6)

One of the richest and most overwhelming passages in the Bible is this discussion of the blessings which are ours *now* in Christ Jesus.

1. *Their Character* (v. 3)

God has blessed us "with all spiritual blessings" (v. 3). The word "spiritual" defines the nature of our blessings. The main idea seems to be that they are spiritual as opposed to natural, material, or temporal. Paul, a childless, landless, homeless man, knew little of blessings of this latter sort, but in regard to spiritual blessings he knew himself to have boundless wealth. The contemplation of these blessings opened in his heart the floodgates of grateful praise. "All spiritual blessings" may be understood in the sense of "every kind of." Whatever our spiritual lives require, God amply and abundantly provides. He has given us "every possible spiritual benefit in Christ!" (v. 3, Phillips).

2. *The Sphere in Which They Are Experienced* (v. 3)

Two expressions define the sphere in which God's people are blessed. One is the phrase, "in heavenly places" (v. 3). This unusual expression occurs five times in Ephesians (1:3, 20; 2:6; 3:10; 6:12, ASV) but nowhere else in the New Testament. To determine its meaning one should study carefully each passage where it is used. In 1:20 it is the sphere to which the risen Christ has been exalted and enthroned; in 2:6 it is the region to which believers have been lifted in fellowship with Christ; in 3:10 it is where principalities and powers learn of the wisdom of God as exhibited through his people; in 6:12 it is the spiritual battleground where believers confront the forces of wickedness. Thus, the phrase "heavenly places" refers not to a physical locality but to a celestial region, a sphere of spiritual activities to which the believer has been lifted in Christ. It is not the heaven of the future but the heaven which lies *even now* within and around the Christian. Believers do indeed belong to two worlds (Phil. 3:20). Temporally they belong to the earth; but spiritually their lives are linked with Christ's, and they belong to the heavenly realm.

The other phrase defining the sphere of Christian blessings is "in Christ" (v. 3). The thought occurs no fewer than twelve times in the first fourteen verses of this epistle. Believers are faithful in Christ, chosen in him, receive grace in him, have their redemption in him, are made a heritage in him, are sealed in him, and so on. Here (v. 3), where it is said that God's people are blessed in Christ, the meaning is that the blessings which they experience come to them by virtue of their union with Christ. He is the great reservoir of blessing, but only those who have living connection with him share in his benefits. To those, however, who do enjoy this vital union God gives the key to his treasures and says in effect, "Go in and take what you will."

3. *The Ground on Which They Come* (vv. 4–6)

These blessings come to us in accordance with an eternal purpose of God (vv. 4–6). The words "according as [i.e., in conformity with the fact that] he hath chosen us" (v. 4) are to be connected in thought with "hath blessed" in verse 3. Paul is saying that salvation has its foundation in an eternal and gracious choice of a sovereign God.

The two key expressions of verses 4–6 are "hath chosen" and "having predestinated." Since all else in the passage revolves around these two ideas, it is absolutely necessary to understand their meanings. The word translated "hath chosen" literally means "to choose out" or "select" (for oneself). It is used in various connections in the New Testament: for example, of Christ's choice of the apostles (Luke 6:13), of the early church's choice of deacons (Acts 6:5), and of the selection of official delegates by the Jerusalem conference (Acts 15:22,25). In the present passage, however, the word relates specifically to the salvation of sinners. It is a key word for what is commonly known as the doctrine of election.

This doctrine magnifies the sovereignty of God, the helplessness of man to save himself, and the sinfulness of sin. It is the very essence of salvation by grace and is intimately bound up with the doctrine of eternal security. In a broad sense, election may be defined as an act of choice whereby God selects an individual or group out of a larger company for a purpose or destiny which he appoints. In a more restricted sense, it is God's gracious and sovereign choice of individual sinners to be saved in and through Christ.

The doctrine of election is often vigorously opposed. Sometimes this opposition arises from a lack of understanding concerning the doctrine. Sometimes it represents a reaction to those who have made the teaching harsh and forbidding. Often, however, the prejudice against election springs from embedded human conceit.

This teaching deals a crushing blow to human pride. It is indeed a leveling doctrine, which strips away all trust in flesh and brings a man to rely wholly on the grace of God in Christ. When rightly understood, election is a precious truth designed to give believers assurance of final salvation and to make them realize how much they owe to God's grace and mercy.

The election of grace receives great emphasis in Paul's epistles (cf. Rom. 8:28 to 11:36; 1 Thess. 1:2–10), but the doctrine is not peculiar to him. The New Testament uniformly teaches that all saving grace in time flows from divine election in eternity. The teaching is regularly brought in, in contexts of praise and devotion and is intended to elicit the adoring gratitude of redeemed people.

Two doctrines—apparently at variance—are taught in the New Testament with respect to salvation. Man has complete freedom of choice. "Whosoever will may come." But the New Testament also affirms, "He hath chosen us."

It has often been said that before his conversion one sees inscribed over the entrance to the narrow way that leads to life eternal the words, "Whosoever will may come." But upon entering he looks back and, to his amazement, sees now the words, "Chosen in him before the foundation of the world." The Bible teaches both human responsibility and divine sovereignty. We must hold to both. To explain an apparent difficulty by denying one or the other of these tenets is to explain away the truth. We may not be able completely to harmonize the two, but we can be sure that they are perfectly harmonized in the mind of God. Let us, in the presence of such profound truth, fall prostrate before God and exclaim with Paul: "O the depth of the riches both of the wisdom and knowledge of God! how unsearchable are his judgments, and his ways past finding out!" (Rom. 11:33).

The other key expression in our passage is the word translated "having predestinated." It literally means "to mark off in advance," then "to foreordain" or "determine before." In the New Testament it is always used of God as determining from eternity. There is probably no rigid distinction between election and predestination; they relate to the same divine act and, for all practical purposes, are identical.

The King James Version attaches the phrase "in love" to the thought of verse 4. Most modern translations favor placing the comma before "in love" and construing these words with "having predestinated" (v. 5). God's predestinating is thus seen to be no harsh and arbitrary act, but rather a gracious and merciful decree made in love. It must be thought of not as a blind, impersonal, and mechanical thing, but as an act of infinite love and wisdom.

(1) *God's choice made in Christ* (v. 4).—God's choice had its ground in Christ. Apart from him and his foreseen work in our behalf there would have been no election and, therefore, no salvation. Since the redemption of sinners is bound up so intimately with the person and work of God's dear Son, no one should assure himself that he is one of God's elect until he knows himself to be in Christ.

(2) *An eternal choice* (v. 4).—God's choice was made "before the foundation of the world." It was an eternal choice; it was made before the beginning of time and before any created thing came into being. The New Testament appears to emphasize this fact in order to bring out that God's choice is immutable, that nothing can happen in time or eternity to shake his determination to save his people.

(3) *A purposeful choice* (vv. 4–5).—God's choice was purposeful. This truth is brought out in two statements. The first, "that we should be holy and without blame before him," expresses the purpose of divine election as to our character. God wanted us to be a certain kind of people; he wanted us to be *holy;* he wanted us to be *blameless.* The two words are really two sides of the same thing.

Barclay points out that the word "holy," which speaks in this context of inner consecration, has in it "the idea of *difference* and of *separation*." His comments are significant. "A temple," he continues, "is *holy* because it is different from other buildings; a priest is *holy* because he is different from ordinary men; a [sacrifice] victim is *holy* because it is different from other animals; God is supremely *holy* because God is different from men; the Sabbath day is *holy* because it is different from other days. So, then, God chose the Christian that he should be *different* from other men." [1] This difference consists in his separation, his dedication to God.

The word that is translated by "without blame" is a sacrificial word. In reference to sacrificial animals it meant "without blemish" or "without defect." Here it denotes the stainless life which God purposes for his people to live.

Observe that the passage does not say in so many words that we are elected to heaven. This idea of course is involved, but it is not exactly what is said. The text says we are chosen to "be holy and without blemish" (ASV). Some people seem eager to go to heaven, but they have no desire for holiness. Yet without holiness "no man shall see the Lord" (Heb. 12:14). (Note that if holiness of life is the end and aim of election, it cannot possibly be the grounds of it. God did not choose us because he saw something good in us which was not present in another. He chose us, undeserving sinners though we were, in order that we might become holy people.)

The second statement of purpose is put in terms of our standing before God: "unto the adoption of children by Jesus Christ" (v. 5). Adoption embraces more than our relationship to God as his children. This relationship we have by the new birth. Used in the New Testament only by Paul, the word "adoption" literally means a "placing as sons." Once (Rom. 9:4) Paul uses it of the covenant relationship between Israel and God, but everywhere else he uses it to emphasize the

privileges which belong to believers. The complete manifestation of our adoption and the full realization of its privileges
are yet future (Rom. 8:23).

(4) *Unto himself* (v. 5).—All of God's saving activity in
regard to sinners is "unto . . . himself." This phrase expresses
the goal of all; that is, to bring sinners, redeemed through
Christ, into an adoring relationship to God as the true end
and object of their being.

(5) *According to his will* (v. 5).—The divine election is
"according to the good pleasure of his will." The ground of
God's choice, of his predestinating us to be his sons, is not
to be found in us but in his own goodness and in the deliberate resolve of his own mind. F. F. Bruce explains: "It was
not because He foresaw something acceptable in us, not even
because he foreknew that we would believe the gospel, that
He singled us out for such an honour as this. The ground must
be sought exclusively in His own gracious character." [2] God's
election is an act of his own pure goodness, of his own benevolent sovereignty. What he did, he did solely because it seemed
right and good for him to do it.

(6) *To exhibit his grace* (v. 6).—The ultimate end of God's
choice, of his foreordination of sinners, is "the praise of the
glory of his grace." The context suggests that "the glory of
his grace" refers to the profuse outpouring of God's grace
"wherein he hath made us accepted in the beloved" (v. 6).
The teaching, then, is that grace has been gloriously manifested and (because of this) is to be eternally praised. "The
design of redemption . . . is to exhibit the grace of God in
such a conspicuous manner as to fill all hearts with wonder
and all lips with praise." [3]

II. AN ENUMERATION OF THE DIVINE BLESSINGS (1:7–14)

All that Paul has said in verses 3–6 constitutes a description of God's blessings to his people. Verses 7–14 enumerate
some of these divine blessings.

1. *Redemption and Forgiveness* (v. 7)

"Redemption" and "the forgiveness of sins [trespasses]" (v. 7) are joined together in such a way as to suggest the closest possible relation, but they are not identical concepts. "Redemption" denotes a release brought about by the payment of a price. Barclay calls attention to the varied uses of the word: of ransoming a slave or a prisoner of war, of releasing a man under penalty of death for some crime, of the emancipation of Israel from Egyptian bondage, and of God's rescuing his people in the time of their trouble. "In every case," he explains, "the conception is the delivering or the setting free of a man from a situation from which he himself was powerless to liberate himself, or from a penalty which he himself could never have paid." [4] In Christ we have been delivered from the shackles of sin, from enslavement to Satan, and from all the misery attendant upon such enslavement.

The ransom price, the means by which this release has been effected, is "his [i.e., Christ's] blood" (v. 7). This sacrificial term calls to mind the blood of victims offered to God in the Old Testament economy. Here the word represents the death of Christ in its character as a sacrifice for sin and is a reminder to us of the infinite price God paid for our redemption.

To the idea of redemption Paul adds that of "the forgiveness of sins." The figure in the Greek word rendered by "sins" is that of a falling by the way, an offence, a trespass. Here the plural signifies the *accumulation* of sinful acts which were chargeable to us. "Forgiveness" means literally "a sending away." (Cf. Psalm 103:11–12.) By putting the phrase "forgiveness of sins" in grammatical apposition with the word "redemption," Paul implies that forgiveness is the central feature of our redemption.

The measure of redemption is expressed in the phrase,

"according to the riches of his grace" (v. 7). God's bequests are in proportion to the abundance of his treasures. He does not give in stinted fashion but with unbounded liberality. If redemption were according to the measure of man's merit, there would be no redemption. But who can measure the wealth of God's grace?

2. *Wisdom and Prudence* (vv. 8–10)

W. T. Conner used to say to his classes that Paul puts emphasis on intelligence in religion. Paul teaches here that not only has God's grace brought redemption and forgiveness; it has overflowed—this is the literal meaning of the word "abound"—in the additional gifts of "wisdom and prudence" (v. 8). Wisdom may be defined as "the knowledge that sees into the heart of things, which knows them as they really are. Prudence is the understanding which leads to right action." [5] The one is intellectual knowledge; the other is practical understanding. One satisfies the mind; the other leads to right conduct.

In giving these gifts Christ bestows upon believers a capacity for comprehending something of God's purpose for the universe—"the mystery of his will . . . which he hath purposed" in Christ (v. 9). The word "mystery" occurs six times in Ephesians (here; 3:3,4,9; 5:32; 6:19) and often elsewhere in the New Testament. It is used of the thoughts and plans of God, which are hidden from human reason and comprehension and must be divinely revealed, if they are to be known at all. It refers to a secret, but one which has been made an *open* secret in the gospel. In Ephesians 3:3–4, 9 "mystery" seems to have special reference to God's eternal purpose of including Gentiles as well as Jews in the scope of Christ's beneficent reign. In 5:32 it speaks of the spiritual union of Christ and his church. In 6:19 "mystery" is practically equated with the gospel. Here (v. 9) it has to do with the secret of God's dealing with the world.

This mystery, which God has made known to us "according to his good pleasure," is defined as follows: "that in the dispensation of the fulness of times he might gather together in one all things in Christ, both which are in heaven, and which are on earth" (vv. 9–10). These words give Paul's description of the scope and content of God's purpose for the universe. In short, it is "the establishment of a new order, a new creation, of which Christ shall be the acknowledged head." [6] Christ already is "head over all things to the church" (1:22); this passage declares it is God's intent that he shall be head of a regathered, reunited universe.

The Greek word behind our word "dispensation" (v. 10) means "stewardship" or "administration" and is used here of the administration, or the carrying out, of God's purpose. The "fulness of the times" (cf. Gal. 4:4) suggests a particular point of time that completes a long prior period. The "dispensation of the fulness of the times" (ASV) thus speaks of the carrying out (administration) of the purpose of God when the time is ripe.

At the end of one appointed period of time God sent forth His Son (Gal. 4. 4); when all the times and seasons which the Father has fixed by His own authority have run their course, God's age-long purpose which he planned in Christ will attain its full fruition. Everything in heaven and earth will then be summed up in Christ. [7]

"That . . . he might gather together in one" (v. 10) translates a Greek word which literally means "to head up" or "to sum up." This word was sometimes used in military affairs to describe the heading up again of scattered troops under the leadership of their commander. "Paul seems to picture all . . . of God's possession as having been scattered in the conflict with the forces of evil. It was his purpose that he would gather up all these scattered holdings and put them under one supreme captain, Jesus Christ." [8]

The expression "all things" (v. 10) is almost a technical phrase equivalent to the totality of creation. This meaning is further defined by the inclusive phrase, "the things in the heavens, and the things upon the earth" (v. 10, ASV). It would be wrong to see this expression as implying ultimate salvation for all people. It rather points in a general way to the restoration of unity and harmony to God's universe. "In Christ" points up the truth that the focal person in this restoration is Jesus Christ. The ultimate destiny of the universe now rests in the hands which once were nailed to the cross.

3. A Heavenly Heritage (vv. 11–12)

Verse 11 in the King James Version reads: "in whom also we have obtained an inheritance," suggesting that God has not only imparted to us a knowledge of his redemptive purpose but has actually made us heirs of its blessings. There is probably an allusion to the experience of Israel in obtaining an inheritance in the Promised Land. Just as each Israelite had his share of that inheritance, so each believer becomes a partaker of the heavenly inheritance which Christ has secured for his people. Understood in this manner, the thought of the passage is quite similar to that in Colossians 1:12: "The Father . . . hath made us meet to be partakers of the inheritance of the saints in light."

However, nearly all recent interpreters favor the translation of verse 11 found in the American Standard Version: "in whom also we were made a heritage." According to this reading, the teaching is not that believers *obtain* an inheritance (though this statement of course is true), but rather that they themselves become *God's* heritage. The allusion is to Israel's peculiar relation to God. Deuteronomy 32:9 declares that "the Lord's portion is his people; Jacob is the lot of his inheritance." Paul sees the spiritual counterpart of this idea in the relation of Christians to God. They are now God's special possession; they are his chosen people.

God's aim in making believers his possession is expressed by the words, "that we should be to the praise of his glory"

(v. 12). It is not that believers might take pride in their position and boast of their special privileges. (Israel had made this mistake in interpreting their relation to God and his purpose.) The aim is rather to the end that, through believers, God's glory might come to be seen and adored.

Observe the words, "we who . . . before hoped in Christ" (ASV). These words suggest that in verses 11–12 Paul had especially in mind Jewish believers whose hope was fixed on the Messiah before he came, and "who accepted Him when He appeared either immediately (like the original disciples) or after an interval (like Paul himself)." [9] The conversion of Jews who before hoped in the Messiah was thus the first stage in the realization of God's purpose to bring all the subjects of redemption into one harmonious body (cf. v. 10). The second stage is implied in verses 13–14, where Paul shows that Gentile Christians ("ye also," v. 13) are included in that same comprehensive purpose.

4. *The Gift of the Spirit* (vv. 13–14)

The gift of the Spirit is to be distinguished from the gifts of the Spirit. The latter are special endowments bestowed by the Spirit; but the former is the Spirit himself, given by the Father through Christ (cf. Acts 2:38; 1 Cor. 12:4ff). The word "gift" does not occur in this passage, but Paul clearly had in mind the bestowal of the Spirit upon believers—the final blessing in the enumeration begun at verse 7.

The main thought of verses 13–14 centers around the Holy Spirit and the significance of his presence in the life of believers. The manner in which he is referred to ("that holy Spirit of promise") is worthy of note. The Spirit is in himself holy, and it is his mission and work to make us holy. He is called the "Spirit of promise" because his coming was the fulfilment of promise, his manifestation at Pentecost and his ministry with believers having been predicted by the prophets (cf. Joel 2:28) and reaffirmed by Christ.

Two figures are used by the apostle to point up the significance of the gift of the Spirit. First, there is the figure of a *seal*. Believers are "sealed with" the Holy Spirit (cf. v. 13 and 4:30). The commentaries list three uses of the seal: to authenticate as genuine, to render secure, and to denote ownership. In all these senses believers are sealed, but the primary idea in the present passage appears to be the last named. Thus, when Paul affirms that Gentile believers have been sealed with the Holy Spirit, he is saying that the presence of the Spirit in their lives is the token or proof that they, as truly as Jewish believers, belong to God. (Compare this point with the thought in vv. 11–12 about being made a heritage.)

The other figure used is that of an *earnest*. The Holy Spirit is "the earnest of our inheritance" (v. 14). (Note the use of the pronoun "our," by which Paul includes both Jewish and Gentile believers as sharing a common experience.) The word translated "earnest" was a legal and commercial term used of a deposit, a first instalment, a down payment. (The same word is used in modern Greek for an engagement ring.) The word is used here in the sense of a pledge or a guarantee. The presence of the Spirit in the believer's life is God's pledge that the Christian will one day have complete redemption and will enjoy in all its fulness the inheritance laid up for him. But there is a further suggestion in the use of this word. The earnest was itself a part of the purchase price, the same in kind as the full payment. The obvious inference is that our present experience of the Holy Spirit is a foretaste of the joys and blessedness of the life to come.

The phrase "until the redemption of the purchased possession" (v. 14) expresses the purpose of the sealing. The "purchased possession" must be understood as referring to God's people (cf. 1 Peter 2:9), and the "redemption" in view is the full completion of redemption. There is, of course, a sense in which believers already are redeemed; but there is another sense in which redemption is yet future, for at present our redemption is incomplete. It will not be complete until we each have a resurrected and glorified body and stand before God without blemish. The presence of the Spirit in our lives guarantees that what God has begun he will in due time accomplish fully.

A second and ultimate purpose in the sealing of the Spirit is expressed in the words, "unto the praise of his glory" (v. 14). The phrase speaks of the adoring confession of God's excellence that shall one day be made when the redemption of his people is consummated.

ACTIVITIES FOR ENRICHMENT

Read aloud the doxology (vv. 3–14), letting your voice give emphasis to the meaning you now see in the words.

C. H. Spurgeon used the idea, "The Checkbook of Faith," to set forth concepts of a believer's blessings in Christ. If you were to represent each of the blessings discussed in this chapter by a check form, decide what you would indicate for the time, place, payer, and payee. Name the blessings which might be filled in as representing the amount of each check.

In a sense, these checks come to each believer daily. They are useless unless cashed. Are you cashing yours? Or, are you living like a spiritual pauper when you really possess "all spiritual blessings . . . in Christ Jesus"?

----

[1] William Barclay, *The Letters to the Galatians and Ephesians* (Philadelphia: The Westminster Press, 1958), p. 89.

[2] F. F. Bruce, *The Epistle to the Ephesians* (New York: Fleming H. Revell Company, 1961), pp. 29–30.

[3] Charles Hodge, *A Commentary on the Epistle to the Ephesians* (Grand Rapids: Wm. B. Eerdmans Publishing Company, 1950), p. 38.

[4] Barclay, *op. cit.*, p. 93.

[5] J. Armitage Robinson, *St. Paul's Epistle to the Ephesians* (London: Macmillan and Company, 1909), p. 30. Used with permission of Macmillan & Company, Ltd., and St. Martin's Press, Inc. U.S.A.

[6] Bruce, *op. cit.*, p. 32.

[7] *Ibid.*, p. 33.

[8] Ray Summers, *Ephesians: Pattern for Christian Living* (Nashville: Broadman Press, 1960), p. 21.

[9] Bruce, *op. cit.*, pp. 34–35.

CHAPTER 3

The Resources of God's New People:

A Prayer

Ephesians 1:15–23

PAUL'S PRAYERS are in some respects the high watermark of his epistles. Nowhere else, Maclaren observes, "do his words come more winged and fast, or his spirit glow with greater fervour of affection and holy desire than in his petitions for his friends."[1] With some people prayer appears to be an unpleasant duty; with Paul it was obviously a supreme joy.

This particular prayer is by no means an ordinary one, for it is replete with profound spiritual truth. In fact, so full of instruction is this passage that it is difficult to know where the prayer ends and the distinctly instructive portion of the epistle begins. Many interpreters would arbitrarily make the break at the end of verse 19, but it is better to retain verses 15–23 as a unit.

I. THE OCCASION FOR THE PRAYER (1:15)

Paul's prayer reveals something of his deep concern for the Christians to whom he was writing and of his deep joy in the work of grace which they had expressed.

1. *The Readers' Experience of Divine Grace*

Paul's prayer was first prompted by the amazing display of divine grace in the readers' lives. This idea is suggested by the word "wherefore" (v. 15), which points back in a general way to the great truths expounded in verses 3–14.

More particularly it refers to the thought of verses 13–14, where Paul has set out the signal manifestation of God's grace in sealing the Gentile believers with the Holy Spirit. Present attainments in grace give occasion for gratitude and afford encouragement to believe that yet greater blessings may be had from the hand of God.

2. *The Report of the Readers' Faith and Love*

The second occasion for this prayer is brought out in the words, "after I heard of your faith in the Lord Jesus, and love unto all the saints" (v. 15). The report of his readers' spiritual condition moved Paul to prayer on their behalf. "Faith" and "love," two great words which denote the leading graces of Christian character, sum up the believers' experience. Their faith is in the Lord Jesus; their love is manifested toward all the saints.

Some scholars have inferred from the words "after I heard" that Paul had had no personal acquaintance with the readers of this letter and that they therefore could not have been his converts. This interpretation, however, misses the point. The words are not speaking of the initial experience of conversion. Rather, they describe a present and continuing experience of trust and devotion.

II. THE SUBSTANCE OF THE PRAYER (1:16–19a)

The prayer has two main themes: thanksgiving and intercession. It applies to the immediate recipients of the letter, but may it not also be a sample of the requests that the Holy Spirit makes in his prayers for us? (See Rom. 8:26.)

1. *Thanksgiving* (v. 16)

Paul's prayer is, first, one of thanksgiving. The word for "give thanks" (v. 16) is characteristically Pauline, being found in his writings twenty-six times. In his letter to the Romans, for example, he thanks God that their "faith is spoken of throughout the whole world" (1:8). In 1 Corinthians he writes of his gratitude "for the grace of God which was given you in Christ Jesus" (1:4, ASV). And he thanks God "upon every remembrance of" the Philippians (Phil. 1:3).

Three things may be said about the thanksgiving of Paul as expressed in the present passage. First, that for which he is especially grateful is the good news of the faith and love of the readers. Second, his gratitude is constant and continual ("I cease not"). Third, it is addressed to God. Thus does the apostle recognize that God is the true fountain of all that is good in his people.

2. Petition (vv. 17–19a)

This prayer is mainly one of petition or intercession. The burden of it is "that the God of our Lord Jesus Christ, the Father of glory, may give unto you the spirit of wisdom and revelation . . . that ye may know . . ." (vv. 17–18). Observe that the person to whom the prayer is addressed is designated as "the God of our Lord Jesus Christ, the Father of glory." From this sublime title we learn that Paul's approach to God had nothing of thoughtless and irreverent familiarity about it. And we would do well to imitate him in this respect. When we go to God in prayer there ought to be a profound reverence, a sense of deep and inexpressible wonder. Furthermore, the title reveals something of the encouragement Paul found to pray. It was not to a far-off and unknown deity that he unburdened his heart; it was to "the God of our Lord Jesus Christ." To think of God in this way is to be reminded that in approaching God in prayer we in truth draw near to a "throne of grace."

To speak of God as "the God of our Lord Jesus Christ" in no sense detracts from the uniqueness of Christ. God is the God of Christ in the sense that he is the God whose work Christ came to perform and by whom Christ was sent into the world. To speak of God as "the Father of glory" is to declare he is the Father who possesses glory, the Father of whom glory is a characteristic feature.

The prayer takes the form of a single definite request: that "the Father . . . may give unto you the spirit of wisdom and revelation" (v. 17). And this request is for a definite end: "that ye may know . . ." (v. 18).

The "spirit of wisdom" is often interpreted as an attitude of mind, as when we speak of a spirit of meekness or of courage. Understood in this fashion the words express a desire of the apostle that his readers may have an attitude of mind, a spiritual disposition, by which they will be able to comprehend divine truth. This interpretation is apparently the one the translators of the King James Version followed, for the word "spirit" is not capitalized. However, probably it should be capitalized as a reference to the Holy Spirit. If such be done the verse is seen as a prayer for the readers to experience to the fullest degree the blessed ministry of the Spirit—particularly in his capacity as "Spirit of wisdom and revelation." Apart from the illumination produced by this ministry of the Spirit there can be no understanding of divine truth.

Observe that the knowledge of which Paul speaks is not simply a knowledge of things or facts; it is knowledge—the Greek word denotes accurate, thorough knowledge—which concerns God ("in the knowledge of him," v. 17). Such knowledge requires that "the eyes of . . . [one's] understanding" be "enlightened" (v. 18). With these words the apostle explains the last part of verse 17. That is, to have the Spirit of wisdom and revelation is to have the eyes of one's understanding ("heart," ASV) enlightened. In Paul's writings "heart" stands for the whole inner man. Its use here reminds us that the illumination needed is inward and spiritual.

"That ye may know" (v. 18) introduces the three specific elements of knowledge which Paul desires his readers to possess: "the hope of his calling" (v. 18), "the riches of the glory of his inheritance in the saints" (v. 18), and "the exceeding greatness of his power to us-ward who believe" (v. 19). Note that it is God's calling, God's inheritance, and God's power. But more specifically, it is the *hope* of his calling, the *glory* of his inheritance, and the *greatness* of his power which Paul wants the readers to grasp and appreciate.

(1) *The hope of his calling* (*v. 18*).—The "calling," which looks to the past, is God's in the sense that he extended it to us. The reference is not merely to a general invitation to salvation; the word denotes the effectual call of God that actually issues in conversion. This is the uniform meaning of the word in the epistles of Paul, for the called of God, in his view, are those who have obeyed God's summons and have been made believers in Christ.

This divine call involves a "hope," and it is a knowledge of this that Paul desires for his readers. The word "hope" is used in two different ways in the Scriptures. It may be used objectively for the things hoped for. Colossians 1:5 is an example: "the hope which is laid up for you in heaven." If taken in this sense, hope speaks of the outcome or issue of redemption, the ultimate consummation of the purpose of God as it respects his people. In praying that his readers may "know" this hope, Paul is asking not only that they may know what it really and essentially is but that they may understand something of its compass and scope. It is possible that this interpretation is the one to be given to this passage.

Sometimes, however, the word "hope" is used in a subjective sense of an expectant attitude, the emotion of hope. For example, note 1 Peter 1:13: "Set your hope perfectly on the grace that is to be brought unto you at the revelation of Jesus Christ" (ASV). The same meaning is to be given to the word in Romans 5:2: "We rejoice in hope of the glory of God" (ASV). To "know" hope in this sense is to have conscious experience of it.

It is quite possible that there is in this passage a blending of both the subjective and the objective ideas. This view is held by Scroggie, who says that Paul's prayer is "that we may know in happy experience the expectation which God's saving calling of us has begotten in our souls; and that we may know also what that calling has secured for us, and reserves for us in the heavenly life which awaits us."

(2) *"The riches of the glory of his inheritance in the saints"* (*v. 18*).—These words also are capable of more than one interpretation. The main question is whether the reference is to *God's* inheritance in the saints or to the *saints'* inheritance in God. The former view is very widely held and has much to commend it. On the surface it appears to be the more obvious interpretation. The text does not speak of our inheritance in God, but of "his inheritance in the saints." And verses 11 ("we were made a heritage," asv) and 14 ("the purchased possession") have already made reference to this idea.

Viewed in this manner, the text expresses Paul's desire that believers may know how precious they are to God and what God expects of and from them. He has taken them to be his everlasting portion and has made them wondrous trophies of his grace and power. Our treasure is in God, and in a very true sense his treasure is in his redeemed people. Bruce, who subscribes to this interpretation, points out that "we can scarcely realize what it must mean to God to see His purpose complete, to see creatures of His hand, sinners redeemed by His grace, reflecting His own glory." [3]

Many students, however, feel constrained to interpret the passage as a reference to the saints' inheritance in God. One argument is that it is easy to conceive of our inheritance in God as rich in glory, but difficult to think of the heritage he has in us in this way. Accordingly, it is felt that the inheritance refers to the future glory of believers, the pronoun "his" being understood to denote origin. The inheritance is "his" in the sense that it originates in God and is given by him to his people. "In the saints" must refer to the manner in which the inheritance is distributed among them, with an allusion to the partitioning of the Promised Land among the Israelites of old. This interpretation re-emphasizes the idea of knowing by experience that which we have received by God's grace. (Compare the thought in Joshua 1:3.)

Before passing from this phrase, observe that it is not simply a knowledge of the inheritance for which Paul makes request. His petition is that his readers may know the wealth of the glory of it.

(3) *The exceeding greatness of his power* (*v. 19*).—The "call" referred to the past; the "inheritance" points to the future; the "power," which suggests the limitless resources available to believers, concerns the present. Realizing that the very thought of the glorious wealth of the inheritance held out for Christians may tend to quench rather than stimulate hope of entering into it, Paul wants to inform his readers of the surpassing greatness of God's power at work in them. It is this operative power which brings the fulfilment of the hope and makes possible the realization of the inheritance. Paul does not ask simply that the readers may know the power of God; he wants them to know "the exceeding greatness" of it.

III. THE EXPANSION OF THE PRAYER (1:19*b*–23)

There is a turn in thought at verse 19*b*. The prayer continues, but it is expanded and enlarged so as to take on an informative character.

1. *The Measure of God's Power* (v. 19)

Something of the measure of God's power is brought out by the remarkable accumulation of terms (v. 19, ASV): "exceeding greatness," "power" (Greek, *dunamis*), "working" (Greek, *energeia*), "strength" (Greek, *kratos*), "might" (Greek, *ischus*). The heaping up of words suggests the idea of power, the very telling of which exhausts the resources of language and finally defies description.

2. The Supreme Demonstration of God's Power
(vv. 20–23)

Even if this power is beyond description, Paul can nonetheless point to the supreme demonstration of it in the person of Christ. It is described as the "working of the strength" of God's might "which he wrought in Christ, when he raised him from the dead" (vv. 19–20, ASV). God's power at work in believers is none other than resurrection power. It is the power that raised Christ from the dead, seated him at God's right hand, and gave him supremacy over all the universe. What tremendous encouragement this truth should give to believers! The power available to us in daily living is not to be conceived of as a tiny brook, barely meeting the demands made upon it. It is like a surging river, driving before itself all the obstacles it may encounter.

In the development of this theme Paul makes three far-reaching affirmations about Christ, or more exactly, about what God has done in and for Christ. The pivotal expressions are: "He raised . . . and made him to sit" (v. 20, ASV); "he put . . . in subjection" (v. 22a, ASV); and "gave him to be head" (v. 22b, ASV).

(1) *The resurrection and exaltation of Christ* (*vv. 20–21*).— The raising of Christ from the dead and his exaltation to the right hand of God are attributed specifically to the exertion of God's mighty power. ("Raised" and "set" are, in the Greek, participles modifying the finite verb, "he wrought.") The two things are really two stages of one epochal event.

The resurrection of Christ, the fact of which was vigorously and joyously proclaimed by the apostles, is a matter of supreme importance. It authenticated the Lord's ministry, sealed his redemptive work, marked the beginning of his glorification, and was a public attestation of the Father's acceptance of his sacrifice. Moreover, it provides the dynamic, the power, for Christian living and is the pattern and pledge of the believer's resurrection. Since Christ has "become the firstfruits of them that slept" (1 Cor. 15:20), we therefore confidently await the hour when he "shall fashion anew the body of our humiliation, that it may be conformed to the body of his glory" (Phil. 3:21, ASV).

Having raised Christ from the dead, God further exhibited his power by setting him "at his own right hand" (vv. 20–21). These words speak of the exaltation or enthronement of Christ. The reference to the "right hand" of God is a figurative expression for the place of supreme privilege and authority. Paul proceeds to declare that Christ is enthroned "far above all rule, and authority, and power, and dominion, and every name that is named" (v. 21, ASV). Likely, his words refer to various ranks and orders of celestial greatness among angelic beings, but it is not necessary to draw fine lines of distinction between the terms. They are brought together to express the unique supremacy and sovereign power of Jesus Christ.

The obvious meaning is that whatever kinds of rulership there may be and whatever names they may bear, they must acknowledge and submit to the supremacy of him to whom God has given "the name which is above every name" (Phil. 2:9). This sovereign and unshared supremacy of Christ holds true "not only in this world [age], but also in that which is to come" (v. 21). Above all grades of rulership, real or imagined, good or evil, present or future, the invincible power of God has exalted and enthroned the crucified and risen Christ.

(2) *The universal dominion of Christ* (v. 22).—God has not only exalted Christ above all created beings, he also has given him universal dominion. Two great deeds of God are in view: He wrought his power in raising and exalting Christ and he subjected all things to him. As has been pointed out, "raised" and "set" (v. 20) are participles qualifying the expression "he wrought." But "hath put" (v. 22) is a verb in finite form, co-ordinate with "wrought" of verse 20.

This dominion of Christ is brought out in verse 22: He "hath put all things under his feet." These words, found also in Hebrews 2:8, are quoted from Psalm 8:6. In the psalm they speak of man and the dominion God intended him to have. Here, with the suggestion that God's ideal for man has been realized in Christ, they graphically depict the placing of all things under his sovereign lordship. The reference to all things being "put under" Christ's feet means that all things are arranged under him, subordinated to him. The words imply absolute subjection, but their complete fulfilment, as brought out in 1 Corinthians 15:27, will not come until death itself is destroyed. Christ's present enthronement at God's right hand, however, is the pledge that such will come to pass.

(3) *The headship of Christ over the church* (*vv. 22–23*).—God has established a unique relationship between Christ and the church. He "gave him to be head over all things to the church" (ASV). There are two lines of interpretation of this statement. One takes the verb "gave" quite literally and construes "to the church" with it. Accordingly, Christ is seen as in some sense *God's gift to the church*. It is an astounding statement, and a concept that staggers the imagination. This exalted, sovereign Christ a gracious gift of God to his redeemed people—what a stupendous Gift!

Those who advocate this interpretation further suggest that God gave Christ to the church in a certain capacity. The verse might be translated, "He gave him, as head over all things, to the church." Thus understood, "head over all things" repeats the substance of "hath put all things under his feet" and simply restates the thought of Christ's absolute and supreme dominion over all the universe. In this interpretation, then, the headship of Christ over the church is not explicitly stated. The idea is implied, however, by the statements which follow, especially in the reference to the church as "his body" (v. 23).

The other line of interpretation attaches to the verb "gave"

the somewhat weakened meaning of "appointed." Furthermore, those who advocate this view construe the words "head
over all things" more intimately with "to the church," and
interpret these latter words in the sense of "with reference
to the church." Thus God "gave [appointed] him to be head
over all things [i.e., supreme head] with reference to the
church." In this view there is an explicit, not simply an implied, teaching of the headship of Christ over the church.
This headship, however, is still admittedly a part of the larger
concept of the universal dominion of Christ set forth in the
preceding verses.

But however one interprets the details of the passage, the
over-all impression is that of Christ's sovereign authority over
his people and that of the vital unity which exists between
him and them.

The highly significant word "church," used here in Ephesians for the first time, occurs with unusual frequency in the
epistle. In 3:10 the church is referred to as the means by
which celestial beings learn of "the manifold wisdom of God."
In 3:21 glory is to redound to God "in the church ... throughout all ages, world without end." In the fifth chapter, where
the word is used six times (vv. 23,24,25,27,29,32), the church
is described as the bride of Christ, loved by him, redeemed
by him, and subject to him.

The Greek word (*ekklesia*) translated "church" was used
by the ancients of an assembly, or a legal meeting of citizens,
called out by a herald. In the Greek translation of the Old
Testament this word is sometimes used of the solemn religious assemblies of Israel. When used in a Christian sense, it
means a company of believers, an assembly of called-out
people.

In the New Testament by far the most frequent use of the
word *ekklesia*, "church," is for a local and organized company
of believers joined together for worship, service, and fellowship—for example, the "church of the Thessalonians" (1

Thess. 1:1), the "churches of Galatia" (Gal. 1:2), and so on. Indeed, out of a total of one hundred fifteen occurrences of the word "church," at least ninety to a hundred of them must be interpreted in a local sense. In Ephesians, however, the word "church" seems not to be confined to a local assembly but to be given its most comprehensive and general sense. It goes beyond the concept of a concrete institution or outward, visible organization to that of a great spiritual fellowship including all of the redeemed.

Two profound statements are made about the church in verse 23. First, it is said to be "his [Christ's] body." By speaking of the community of the redeemed in this fashion emphasis is placed on the idea of the vital union of Christ and his people. Together they constitute one organism, each, in a sense, being incomplete without the other. Moreover, there may be the added suggestion that believers exist not simply to enjoy a mystic union with Christ but to be of practical service to him. He, as their head, is the source of their life and power; and they, as his body, are the means by which he effects his purposes.

Second, the church is said to be "the fulness of him that filleth all in all." (A few scholars see this phrase as a description of Christ. He, it is said, is the fulness of God, who fills all in all. [Compare Col. 1:19; 2:9.] Most interpreters, however, feel that the context requires the word "fulness" to be seen as a description of the church.) The thought seems to be, according to some, that the church as Christ's body is *filled by him*. This is the view of Salmond, who explains it to mean that the church is "pervaded by His presence, animated by His life, filled with His gifts and energies and graces." [4] It thereby receives from Christ all that it requires for the realization of its calling and the accomplishment of its mission. Others think that the phrase continues the figure of the body and therefore take it to mean that *the church fills*

Christ. That is to say, the church as Christ's body is the complement of him. *NO*

ACTIVITIES FOR ENRICHMENT

Read and reread the prayer in verses 15–23. Let various class members read it in their favorite translations. Remember that the Holy Spirit inspired this prayer of Paul for his Ephesian friends. It is thus a sample of the prayer that the Holy Spirit offers for each believer (Rom. 8:26). In your private meditations read the prayer as the Holy Spirit's intercession for you.

Word as a separate statement each request involved in the prayer. Think of what the granting of that request will mean in your own life. Meditate on the power available to bring to pass for you the requests involved in this prayer.

---

[1] Alexander Maclaren, *Expositions of Holy Scripture* (Grand Rapids: Wm. B. Eerdmans Publishing Company, 1942), XVI, 52.

[2] W. Graham Scroggie, *Paul's Prison Prayers* (London: Pickering and Inglis, Ltd., n. d.), p. 52.

[3] F. F. Bruce, *The Epistle to the Ephesians* (New York: Fleming H. Revell Company, 1961), p. 40.

[4] S. D. F. Salmond, *The Expositor's Greek Testament* (Grand Rapids: Wm. B. Eerdmans Publishing Company, n. d.), III, 282.

CHAPTER 4

I. THE STATE BEFORE CONVERSION (2 : 1–3)
    1. Deadness (v. 1)
    2. Enslavement to Evil (vv. 2–3a)
       (1) Walking in trespasses and sins (v. 2a)
       (2) Conformed to the standards of the world (v. 2b)
       (3) Ruled over by Satan (v. 2c)
       (4) At the mercy of their passions (v. 3a)
    3. Objects of Divine Wrath (v. 3b)

II. THE CHRISTIAN POSITION (2 : 4–6)
    1. Objects of Divine Mercy (v. 4)
    2. Resurrected to New Life (vv. 5–6)
    3. Fellowship with the Living Christ (vv. 5–6)

III. THE DIVINE PURPOSE (2 : 7–10)
    1. To Exhibit the Wealth of Divine Grace (vv. 7–9)
    2. To Make Possible a Life of Good Works (v. 10)

4

The Formation of God's New People:

By the Quickening of Individuals Dead in Sin

Ephesians 2:1–10

THE OPENING CHAPTER of Ephesians took us back to the counsels of God and let us see how God purposed from eternity to call out in Christ a people for himself—a new, redeemed humanity. This new people of God has Christ for its head, and it constitutes his body. The second chapter of Ephesians tells how, in time, God is actually creating this redeemed society. Two things are stressed: (1) The new humanity is created by the spiritual resurrection of believers (vv. 1–10). (2) The creation of this new humanity involves the uniting of believing Jews and believing Gentiles into one spiritual body (vv. 11–22).

In Ephesians 1:20–23 Paul describes the mighty power of God in raising Christ from the dead and giving him universal dominion. In 2:1–10 he says that same power is at work in raising believers from the death of sin and lifting them to the "heavenly places" in Christ.

In the Greek text the first seven verses are one long and involved sentence. The main verb (translated "hath quickened") is not reached until verse 5. The two leading ideas are: "You . . . were dead" (v. 1), and "God . . . hath quickened" (vv. 4–5). The whole paragraph is a sort of spiritual biography describing what believers once were apart from Christ, what they have become in Christ, and God's purpose in effecting this remarkable transformation.

I. THE STATE BEFORE CONVERSION (2:1–3)

Paul sets forth the pre-Christian state of his readers, in order to emphasize the magnitude of both the power and the mercy which they have experienced. The description of their former life becomes a sort of foil against which the amazing power and grace of God stand out in brilliant relief. Three frightening indictments are made: They were dead (v. 1); they were enslaved to evil (vv. 2–3a); they were objects of divine wrath (v. 3b).

1. *Deadness* (v. 1)

The idea of deadness suggests the sinner's alienation from God, the source of life, and emphasizes his utter helplessness to save himself. The unregenerate are spiritually dead, void of all true spiritual life. The nature of this death is explained by the words "in trespasses and sins." The word for "trespasses" represents sin as a fall, a false step, an offence. It suggests losing one's way or straying from the right road. The word for "sin," which is the more common New Testament term, represents sin as a missing the mark, a failure to measure up to God's standard.

The reading, "through your trespasses and sins" (ASV), assigns the cause of the deadness. It is as though the whole world were one vast graveyard and every gravestone had the same inscription, "Dead through sin." All died of the same dread disease. The manifestations of this death are seen in the moral decay, the spiritual blindness, and the total indifference to the things of God which characterize the unregenerate.

2. *Enslavement to Evil* (vv. 2–3a)

Verses 2–3a contain two leading statements, one specifically naming the Gentile readers of this letter ("ye," v. 2), the other more general and including Paul and his fellow Jews ("we all," v. 3). Within these two statements, however, there are four separate ideas. They vividly depict a state of moral degradation and spiritual enslavement.

(1) *Walking in trespasses and sins* (*v.* 2a).—This spiritual enslavement is brought out first by a reference to the sphere within which the readers had lived and moved in their pre-Christian days. They are reminded that "in time past" they had "walked" in trespasses and sins. The word "walk"—a common one in the New Testament—is here used ethically for the walk of life, the whole of one's manner of living. Trespasses and sins formed the very atmosphere in which these people once lived (cf. Rom. 1:18–32).

(2) *Conformed to the standards of the world* (*v.* 2b).— The standard to which the readers' lives had conformed prior to their conversion is expressed in the words "according to the course [age] of this world" (v. 2). The phrase is practically equivalent here to "the worldly fashion of the day." To walk according to this fashion is to conform to the world's shifting standards of right and wrong, to be swept up in its pleasures and its practices.

(3) *Ruled over by Satan* (*v.* 2c).—In their pre-Christian life the readers were under the power and dominion of Satan, who is here called the "prince of the power of the air" (v. 2). "Their life was determined and shaped by the master of all evil, the supreme ruler of all the powers of wickedness."[1] This terrible picture is tragically true of the spiritual bondage of all men who are strangers to God's grace in Christ.

The "power of the air" speaks of the totality of evil powers over whom Satan rules as prince. Some interpreters understand the "air" to refer to the atmosphere about us. Others see in the word "air" an allusion not to the abode of these evil powers but to their nature. They are "of the air" in that they do not belong to the earth; they do not have a corporeal nature. They are superhuman, spiritual beings ruled over by Satan (cf. Eph. 6:12, ASV).

In the King James Version the expression, "the spirit that now worketh in the children of disobedience" (v. 2), is put in apposition with "prince" and is thus construed as an additional description of Satan. There is greater grammatical support, however, for adding the preposition "of" before the words "the spirit." The meaning then is: Satan is the prince of the power of the air; he is also the prince or ruler of the spirit that now works in the children of disobedience. This "spirit" may be understood as what we mean when we speak of the spirit of the age. Thus understood, Paul is saying that the spirit of the age (the evil principle) which is at work in unbelievers is ruled over and controlled by the prince of evil. Some contrast may be intended between the evil spirit at work in non-Christians and the Holy Spirit at work in Christians.

"Children of . . ." is a Hebraic form of expression used to describe or characterize. (Cf. "children of this world" [Luke 16:8; 20:34]; "children of light" [1 Thess. 5:5].) The "children of disobedience" are people whose nature and essential character is disobedience. The word translated "disobedience" is in the Bible always used of disobedience toward God. Here it depicts unregenerate man as in rebellion against the God who made him.

(4) *At the mercy of their passions* (*v.* 3a).—Verse 2 describes the manner in which the Gentile readers had "walked" in their pre-Christian lives. In verse 3 Paul includes himself and his fellow Jews in his indictment, for Gentiles were not the only people who had lived in accordance with the standards of the "children of disobedience." Among them "we all," Jewish as well as Gentile believers, "once lived" (v. 3, ASV). This statement was a tremendous admission for a Jew, once a proud Pharisee, to make; but "Paul seldom misses the opportunity of declaring the universal sinfulness of men, the dire level of corruptness on which all, however they differed in race or privilege, stood."[2]

Paul spells out his point very clearly. All men, prior to the work of redeeming grace in their hearts, live "in the lusts of ... [their] flesh" (v. 3). This statement is simply a way of saying that they are at the mercy of their passions. The word for "lusts" in the present passage speaks of a desire for what is forbidden. The word "flesh" should not be understood in a strictly physical sense; flesh as representing the material side of our being is not necessarily bad. However, sin has infected the flesh, and since this is so, the word "flesh" as used by Paul normally stands for the unregenerate nature. It signifies man as apart from God, and is very fairly represented by the word "self" as used in popular religious language.

Jews and Gentiles alike, prior to meeting God in Christ, habitually carry out "the desires of the flesh and of the mind" (v. 3). The phrase means the desires *produced by* the flesh and the mind. The two sources of evil desire are the unregenerate nature ("flesh") and the perverted thoughts and imaginations of the unrenewed mind (cf. Rom. 8:7).

3. *Objects of Divine Wrath* (v. 3b)

Both Jews and Gentiles, Paul affirms, are "by nature children of wrath" (asv). The expression "children of wrath" describes men as not only worthy of the divine wrath but as actually subject to it. The expression is a Hebraism, and is similar in usage to "children of disobedience" in verse 2.

Many moderns think of God as an easygoing, good-natured, grandfatherly Being. To them the idea of a God of wrath is unthinkable. But both the Old and the New Testaments have much to say about the wrath of God. His wrath is a permanent and consistent element in his nature and is best seen as the reverse side of his holy love. God's wrath represents the divine hostility to all that is evil. It is a personal quality without which God could not be fully righteous. Nor is his wrath inconsistent with his love, for without righteous wrath love easily degenerates into mere sentimentality.

Paul declares that men are children of wrath "by nature." There are interpreters who see these words as simply drawing a marked contrast between what men are in grace and what they are "naturally," apart from grace. Other interpreters contend that the phrase "by nature" describes that which is innate. According to this view, there is a principle of sin in man by nature, and man sins because of that innate principle. Unregenerate men are therefore objects of divine wrath, not merely because of what they have done but also because of what they are. "We are sinners *in grain;* every mother's son learns to be naughty without book." [3]

II. THE CHRISTIAN POSITION (2:4–6)

In a sense, the delineation of verses 1–3 is only preparatory to what is said in verses 4–6. Man's sin and God's wrath serve as the dark background against which the wealth of God's mercy and the greatness of his love and grace shine forth the more brilliantly.

The present passage presents a remarkable contrast in the past and present condition of believers. They are objects of divine mercy (v. 4); they have experienced resurrection to new life (vv. 5–6); they have fellowship with the living Christ (vv. 5–6).

1. *Objects of Divine Mercy* (v. 4)

Two things are emphasized in verse 4. First, God alone was the author of the change that had been wrought in the believers. Second, and more specifically, this change is grounded in the boundless mercy and great love of God. "Mercy" (Greek, *eleos*) speaks of God's compassion and pity for helpless sinners; love (Greek, *agape*) is that divine disposition which sees something infinitely precious in men in spite of their sin. Both of these things move God to deliver man from his sinful predicament.

2. *Resurrected* to New Life (vv. 5–6)

Verse 5 is best translated, "Even when we were dead through our trespasses, [God] made us alive together with Christ" (ASV). With these words Paul resumes the thought of verse 1. The central words are, "hath quickened us together with Christ." To quicken means to make alive, to impart life, the idea being practically equivalent to regeneration.

This quickening took place "even when we were dead through our trespasses." This manner of putting the truth emphasizes both the greatness of God's power and the richness of his mercy. Notwithstanding our miserable condition, even while we were held in the grip of spiritual death, God intervened on our behalf and actually communicated spiritual life to us. "Together with Christ" does not mean that he and we were quickened in the same way. The words express the idea of fellowship. The new life that is ours is not only made possible by Christ; it is shared with him.

To emphasize that the believer's redemption in Christ is given freely, Paul inserts by way of a parenthesis, "By grace ye are saved." "By grace" means we were undeserving sinners with absolutely no claim on the mercy of God. "Ye are saved" translates a tense which views salvation as an act completed in the past but continuous and permanent in its results. The whole clause means that our being brought into a state or condition of salvation was due wholly to the pure, free favor of God. It comes in as a sort of exclamation and shows how anxious Paul was to see that the gratuitous nature of salvation will never be forgotten. The thought is repeated and expanded in verse 8.

Verse 6 continues the concept of life by the words, "and hath raised us up together, and made us sit together . . ." These words amplify and expand the truth of the verb "quickened." The quickening includes the being raised and the being seated with Christ. The being raised and the being seated bring the new life out into manifestation. Christ was quickened before he came out of Joseph's tomb, but his leaving the tomb openly manifested the new resurrection life already his.

Each of these verbs ("quickened," "raised," and "made sit") expresses what God has already done for his people. We accept the truth that the quickening and the resurrection are spiritual realities from the very moment of conversion. But it staggers the imagination to be told that the enthronement with Christ is already an accomplished fact. Paul is presenting the matter from God's point of view, and in the mind of God our position in Christ is fixed and certain.

The key to the blessed experience of the resurrected, enthroned life is really the phrase "in Christ Jesus" (v. 6). In virtue of our union with Christ we share his life and exaltation. In the words of H. C. G. Moule: "We are *beside* Him there upon His seat of victory and dominion, because we are embodied *in* Him, by the Spirit's power and in the bond of faith." [4]

3. *Fellowship with the Living Christ* (vv. 5–6)

Observe the use of the word "together" in verses 5–6. There may be some slight allusion to the experiences believers share with one another, but the word mainly speaks of an association or fellowship which believers have with Christ. The idea is in bold contrast to the description of their former life as lived among, and shared with, "the children of disobedience" (vv. 2–3). Each of the three principal verbs in the Greek is a compound form suggesting association—"made-alive-together-with," "raised-up-together-with," and "made-to-sit-together-with."

Each of these verb phrases should be compared with the parallel phrases concerning Christ, as used in 1:20, where we are told that God "raised" Christ and "set" him at his right hand. The believer, by his union with Christ, shares in what God has done for Christ. The truth is almost too glorious to comprehend. No wonder Paul voiced the prayer in 1:17–18.

III. THE DIVINE PURPOSE (2:7–10)

Why has God done all of this for believers? A part of the answer has already been given. God has done what he did on account of his "great love wherewith he loved us" (v. 4). These words speak specifically of God's *motive* in quickening and raising believers. The full statement of *purpose* must be found in verses 7–10. Two ideas may be discerned. The first is elaborated in verses 7–9. It speaks of God's intention to make believers an eternal display of his grace. The second idea (v. 10) declares that his purpose was to make possible a life of good works on the part of believers. These two ideas are not entirely separate and distinct. The manifestation of God's grace and the holiness of his people are both intended to redound to God's glory.

1. *To Exhibit the Wealth of Divine Grace* (vv. 7–9)

Believers are trophies of God's grace, and it is his design that in them the surpassing wealth of that grace may be forever exhibited. The words "he might shew" (v. 7) translate a Greek word that might be used of a demonstration or an exhibition. That which God intends to demonstrate is the "exceeding riches of his grace" (v. 7). (Paul has previously spoken of the wealth of God's grace [1:7], the wealth of the glory of God's inheritance [1:18], and the wealth of mercy [2:4]. Here the addition of the word "exceeding" points to the superlative greatness of divine grace.) This marvelous demonstration of grace is seen in the "kindness" which God has bestowed upon believers "through [in] Christ Jesus" (v. 7). (Note the piling up of words showing God's benevolent attitude toward men—mercy, love, grace, kindness.)

Some interpreters have applied the phrase, "in the ages to come," to the generations from the time of Paul to the second coming of Christ. It is more likely, however, that the "ages to come" are those that follow the "course of this world" (2:2) and that Paul had in mind the grand display of God's wondrous grace in eternity. The plural heightens the thought of endlessness.

Verses 8–9 are intended to confirm and amplify the statement of verse 7. The thought clusters around three great gospel words: "saved," "grace," and "faith." The first word, when used in a theological sense, as here, speaks of a rescue and suggests the imminent peril from which we have been delivered in Christ. "Ye are saved" is the translation of a perfect tense in Greek. It points to a decisive experience in the past, but it also emphasizes a present condition growing out of that past act. The meaning is: You were saved (at some point in the past) and are now in a state or condition of salvation.

From God's point of view salvation is complete, though on our side it may be seen as in progress. (Cf. 1 Cor. 1:18, where a present progressive tense is used: "are being saved," ASV, margin.) The experience has been likened to that of a man in a shipwreck. From the moment he is taken out of the icy water into the lifeboat, he is a saved man. He may scarcely feel his safety or be relieved from his fears; indeed, there may pass many long hours before his feet touch the dry land and his rescue is complete. Nonetheless, from the moment he is in the boat he is safe.

The phrase, "by grace," which has the place of emphasis in verse 8, expresses the means by which men are saved—not by weeping, not by their own willing, not through their own works or efforts, but by sovereign grace. But what is grace? The word is used more than one hundred fifty times in the New Testament (almost a hundred times by Paul alone) and with a wide variety of meanings. But its basic meaning is that of favor shown to the utterly undeserving. The words "by grace" assert that God was under no obligation to save men, that salvation is a bounty from God, not a reward for merit.

Salvation is by grace, but it is also "through faith." This statement does not teach that faith is a meritorious ground or procuring cause of salvation. It asserts rather that faith is the appropriating means; it is the hand that receives the gift. The word signifies trust or reliance upon. "Faith," says Calvin, "brings a man empty to God, that he may be filled with the blessings of Christ." [5]

To strengthen yet more the thought that salvation is wholly a work of God, the apostle adds, "and that not of yourselves: it is the gift of God: not of works, lest any man should boast" (vv. 8–9). Calvin sums up Paul's meaning as follows:

> In these three phrases,—*not of yourselves,—it is the gift of God,— not of works,*—he [Paul] embraces the substance of his long argument in the Epistles to the Romans and to the Galatians, that righteousness comes to us from the mercy of God alone,—is offered to us in Christ by the gospel,—and is received by faith alone, without the merit of works. [6]

The only word calling for further explanation is the pronoun "that." In the English translation it seems to have its antecedent in the word "faith." The thought would then be that even faith is a gift of God. Theologically this interpretation is quite correct (cf. Phil. 1:29). But from the grammatical point of view "that" here seems to refer to the whole process of salvation (i.e., the entire thought of v. 8), which, of course, includes faith. Since salvation is so completely God's work and since human achievement is so conclusively ruled out, it is little wonder that there is no room for any man to boast. All praise must be given to God and his grace.

Come, Thou Fount of ev'ry blessing,
  Tune my heart to sing Thy grace;
Streams of mercy, never ceasing,

> Call for songs of loudest praise:
> Teach me some melodious sonnet,
>   Sung by flaming tongues above;
> Praise the mount—I'm fixed upon it—
>   Mount of Thy redeeming love.
>
> O to grace how great a debtor
>   Daily I'm constrained to be!
> Let Thy goodness, like a fetter,
>   Bind my wand'ring heart to Thee:
> Prone to wander, Lord, I feel it,
>   Prone to leave the God I love;
> Here's my heart, O take and seal it,
>   Seal it for Thy courts above.
>   ROBERT ROBINSON

2. *To Make Possible a Life of Good Works* (v. 10)

Verse 10 is designed to enforce and give a reason for the great truth of verses 8–9. Salvation cannot be of works "for" [because, since] believers are themselves the handiwork of God. The word "workmanship" might be used for a work of art, a poem, a masterpiece. All about us we see the works of God's hands. "The heavens declare the glory of God; and the firmament sheweth his handywork" (Psalm 19:1). But God's greatest work, his *masterpiece*, is a new creature in Christ Jesus. "Created in Christ Jesus" brings out the distinctive meaning Paul had in mind. He does not refer to the first creation when he declares us to be God's workmanship. He refers to the new creation which is effected "in [union with] Christ Jesus."

The stress of this entire verse is on the phrase "unto good works." These words express the end which was in view when we were created in Christ. One must distinguish clearly between good works as the ground of salvation and good works as the proof and fruit of salvation. We are not saved *by* good works, but most assuredly we are saved *for* them. These good works God "prepared that we should walk in them" (ASV).

They are not mere accidental attachments. They are a part of God's eternal plan for his people. We are created for them; they are ready for our doing.

ACTIVITIES FOR ENRICHMENT

In a copy of the hymnbook in use in your church, look at some of the hymns listed under "Grace," "Salvation," "Redemption," or similar topics. Let each member of the class take one of these hymns and use a few minutes to look for lines that contain ideas which parallel truths set forth in the Ephesians passage.

[1] S. D. F. Salmond, *The Expositor's Greek Testament* (Grand Rapids: Wm. B. Eerdmans Publishing Company, n.d.), III, 284.

[2] *Ibid.*, p. 285.

[3] E. K. Simpson, "Commentary on the Epistle to the Ephesians," *The New International Commentary on the New Testament* (Grand Rapids: Wm. B. Eerdmans Publishing Company, 1957), p. 49.

[4] H. C. G. Moule, *Ephesian Studies* (New York: Fleming H. Revell Company, n. d.), p. 76.

[5] John Calvin, *Commentaries on the Epistles of Paul to the Galatians and Ephesians,* trans. William Pringle (Grand Rapids: Wm. B. Eerdmans Publishing Company, 1948), p. 227.

[6] *Ibid.*, p. 228.

CHAPTER 5

I. THE FORMER CONDITION OF THE GENTILES (2:11–12)
   1. Objects of Jewish Contempt (v. 11)
   2. Spiritually Bankrupt (v. 12)

II. THE NEW RELATIONSHIP OF THE GENTILES (2:13–22)
   1. Gentile and Jew Reconciled to One Another (vv. 13–15)
   2. Gentile and Jew at Peace with God (vv. 16–18)
   3. Gentile and Jew Sharing the Privileges and Blessings of the Gospel (vv. 19–22)

5

The Formation of God's New People:

By the Reconciliation of
Jew and Gentile in Christ

Ephesians 2:11–22

THE FIRST HALF OF CHAPTER 2 has told of the spiritual death in which both Jew and Gentile were once held and of the quickening which as individuals they experienced. The last half emphasizes the experience of the body of believers and tells how, through the redemption in Christ, Jew and Gentile have been made into "one new man."

The relationship of these two races in the first Christian century may seem to be of little concern to people of the twentieth century, but several considerations make it significant. For one thing, it was a burning issue in the apostle's time. F. F. Bruce observes that "no iron curtain, colour bar, class distinction or national frontier of today is more absolute than the cleavage between Jew and Gentile was in antiquity." He goes on to declare that the transformation which enabled Jew and Gentile to become truly one in Christ was the "greatest triumph of the gospel in the apostolic age." [1]

What is stated in this passage in terms of the reconciliation of Jew and Gentile involves a very precious principle which is of significance for every age. That principle is movingly stated by John Oxenham in the words we often sing:

> In Christ there is no East or West,
> In Him no South or North.

But alas! the words of James Denney, written half a century

ago, are uncomfortably close to being a picture of our time:

Of all Christian truths which are confessed in words, this is that which is most outrageously denied in deed. There is not a Christian church nor a Christian nation in the world which believes heartily in the Atonement as the extinction of privilege, and the levelling up of all men to the same possibility of life in Christ, to the same calling to be saints. The spirit of privilege, in spite of the Cross, is obstinately rooted everywhere even among Christian men.[2]

Ephesians 2:11-22 shows how, even in Paul's day, God's great purpose of unity had already begun to be realized in Christ (cf. 1:10). The wall of partition which had kept the Gentile at a distance had been broken down; in Christ redeemed Jews and redeemed Gentiles, representing the two hostile sections of humanity, had been reconciled to one another; and through him both walked hand in hand into the presence of God.

The paragraph (vv. 11-22) falls quite naturally into two divisions, marked off by the words "in time past" (v. 11) and "but now" (v. 13). The former phrase alludes to the condition of the Gentiles before conversion, the latter refers to their position in Christ.

I. THE FORMER CONDITION OF THE GENTILES (2:11-12)

The first word of verse 11, "wherefore," arrests attention and relates that which follows to the topic of discussion in 2:1-10. In view of their gracious experience of spiritual transformation, the apostle calls upon his Gentile readers to keep on remembering what they once were apart from God's grace. It is most appropriate for all the children of grace to summon themselves to such recollections. To do so is to deepen our appreciation of the mercy and grace of God and make us more thankful, more humble.

The pre-Christian condition of the Gentiles is summed up in two statements: They were objects of Jewish contempt (v. 11) and they were spiritually bankrupt (v. 12).

1. *Objects of Jewish Contempt* (v. 11)

So intense was the Jewish contempt for the Gentile that it was not even lawful for a Jew to render aid to a Gentile woman in her hour of childbirth. The marriage of a Jew to a Gentile was looked upon as the equivalent of death, and the death rites of the Jewish boy or girl were immediately carried out. Even to enter a Gentile house rendered a Jew ceremonially unclean. In verse 11 Paul refers to this abhorrence which the Jews had for Gentiles. They were "Gentiles in the flesh" and were contemptuously referred to as the "Uncircumcision." "In the flesh" is an obvious allusion to circumcision as the outward symbol of Jewish privilege. The very bodies of the Gentiles had proclaimed their pagan character, the outward mark of uncircumcision being a symbol of their irreligion and debasement.

Paul is careful to make it clear, however, that the Jew who would speak so contemptuously of the Gentile was not all that he should have been. The Jews proudly called themselves the "Circumcision," but Paul knew that for them the symbol of their separation was all too often an outward rite void of any true spiritual reality.

2. *Spiritually Bankrupt* (v. 12)

"That at that time" (v. 12) resumes the thought begun with "remember" in verse 11. The readers are asked to remember the true spiritual deprivation involved in their being Gentiles. Paul sums it up in five descriptive phrases.

First, they were "without Christ." The Greek expression might better be translated "apart from the Christ," the idea being that in their former condition they had no connection with the Messiah; they were completely lacking of any true relation to him. For centuries the Jews had cherished the hope of Messiah. Their understanding of his mission might sometimes have been very inadequate, but even in the darkest hours of their history they never doubted that he would come. From this expectation they drew strength and courage. But the Gentiles neither expected nor knew of the Messiah.

Second, they were "aliens from the commonwealth of Israel." The word "aliens" expresses the general idea of separation and estrangement. The "commonwealth of Israel" speaks of the Israelitish nation as the realm or society in which the sovereignty of God took earthly shape and found expression. It was the sphere within which God made himself known to men and entered into relation with them. Gentiles, so long as they were "without Christ," had no part in that order. They were not at home with the people of God. They were outside the circle of God's chosen people.

Third, the Gentiles were "strangers from the covenants of promise." The reference is to the covenants pertaining to the promise of Messiah. The plural "covenants" is used to indicate that the one covenant, originally made with Abraham, was often renewed with, and reaffirmed for, his descendants. The word for "strangers" carries the idea of being foreign to a thing, having no share in it.

Fourth, since they were strangers from the covenants of promise, the Gentiles had "no hope." Paul does not mean that they had no aspirations and desires, for many Gentiles desired better things. There was a deep hunger on the part of many for spiritual deliverance. But mere desire is not hope. Hope is a blending of desire with expectation, and this the Gentile world did not have. "Their future," writes Eadie, "was a night without a star." [3]

The melancholy which had long enshrouded the ancient pagan world had by New Testament times deepened into unrelieved gloom. Life was so full of trouble, so haunted by black destiny, so brief and uncertain that many people felt that the best thing of all was not to be born, and the next best thing was to die. The despair of the ancient Gentile world is aptly described in Matthew Arnold's lines:

On that hard Pagan world disgust
    And secret loathing fell;
Deep weariness and sated lust
    Made human life a hell.

Finally the Gentiles were "without God in the world." To
have no hope for the future is bad enough; to have no God
in the present makes the situation unspeakably tragic. The
Gentiles were not atheists, for they had gods many and lords
many. The apostle means that they did not have the knowledge of, nor any saving relationship to, the one true God. The
"world" may be mentioned in contrast with "commonwealth."
If so, there is stress on the world as evil, as dark and hostile
and under Satan's dominion. In such a world of sin and death,
of shame and sorrow and suffering, Gentiles had no God to
guide, to befriend, to bless, and to save them.

II. THE NEW RELATIONSHIP OF THE GENTILES (2:13-22)

With verse 13 Paul turns from the past to the present. "But
now" contrasts with "at that time" (v. 12). "In Christ Jesus"
is set over against the words "without Christ" (v. 12).

1. *Gentile and Jew Reconciled to One Another* (vv. 13-15)

Once, apart from the Christ, the Gentiles "were far off" (v.
13). Now, by virtue of being "in Christ Jesus," these same people "are made nigh." To be "far off" is simply a way of restat-
ing in a summary fashion all that Paul had said of the Gentiles
in verses 11-12. Israel, by virtue of their covenant relationship
to God, enjoyed nearness to him; the Gentiles lived at a distance, being alienated from God and separated from his people.

The being "made nigh" appears on the surface to relate
exclusively to the Gentiles' being brought near to God. This
idea undoubtedly is the primary meaning, for both Jew and
Gentile must draw near to God before they can draw near
to one another. However, both nearness to God and incorpo-

ration among his people are included in the words. In verses 14–15 the thought definitely centers in the relationship of Jew and Gentile to one another.

The means by which this new relationship is effected is stated in verse 13*b* and confirmed and explained in verses 14–15 (note "for," v. 14). It is the sacrificial death of Jesus that changes the farness of the Gentile into nearness. Christ has achieved this nearness by abolishing "the law of commandments" which stood as a dividing wall between Jew and Gentile. "The apostle's object is to show that by the death of Christ the exclusiveness of the theocracy was abolished, that Jew and Gentile, by the abrogation of the Mosaic law, are placed on the same level, and that both, in the blood of Christ, are reconciled to God." [4]

The passage bristles with exegetical difficulties, but limited space will not permit discussion of all of them. Only those which are most essential to a correct interpretation can be treated.

In his death Christ "made both" Jew and Gentile "one" and broke down "the middle wall of partition" between them (v. 14). "Both" refers to the two races, Jew and Gentile. "One" in Greek is a neuter word conveying the thought that Christ in his death made these two antagonistic parties a unity. They are "not changed in race, nor amalgamated in blood, but they are 'one' in point of privilege and position toward God." [5]

The "middle wall of partition" is a figurative description of the barrier that existed between Jew and Gentile. Likely there is an allusion to the wall in the Jerusalem Temple which separated the court of the Gentiles from the sanctuary proper. At various places along this wall there were signs in Hebrew and Greek forbidding Gentiles to pass beyond it on pain of death. That barrier with its inscribed stones was still standing when Paul wrote Ephesians, and he used it as a tangible symbol of the enmity which separated Jew and Gentile.

In the King James Version, the word, "enmity" (v. 15) is

taken with the words that follow it. In the Greek text the word for "enmity" may be understood as being in apposition with the expression, "the middle wall." Thus, the meaning is that the wall is the hostility existing between Jew and Gentile—and all such racial hostilities of all times.

The dividing wall of hostility between the two races was removed when Christ "in his flesh" (i.e., his incarnate state, and especially the death he endured in that state) abolished the "law of commandments" (v. 15). Thus, the law is seen as in some sense being a hindrance to unity between Jew and Gentile. The legal system embodied in the law of Moses was of divine origin and was intended to protect Israel from the paganism of surrounding nations. Yet this system, misinterpreted and abused, in time became a source of Jewish pride and exclusiveness in relation to the Gentiles. "Having abolished" translates a participle which modifies "hath broken down." It tells the means by which the middle wall was destroyed. The word itself means to make ineffective or to nullify, the thought here being that Christ has abrogated the law.

The question naturally arises: In what sense has the law been abrogated? Some interpreters see in the statement a reference to the setting aside of the ceremonial law because of the fulfilment in Christ of all that it typified. Others understand the reference to be to the whole Mosaic law. Paul's definition appears to lend support to the latter view. He calls it "the law of commandments contained in [expressed by] ordinances [decrees]" (v. 15). The thought is of an elaborate system or code ("law") comprised of minute regulations and prescriptions ("commandments") and expressed by, or couched in, revealed edicts ("decrees"). Such a legal system is viewed as a barrier between the two racial groups, and Christ has rendered it inoperative by his death.

A similar idea is in Colossians 2:14, where Paul declares that Christ has blotted out "the handwriting [bond of indebtedness] . . . that was against us, . . . nailing it to his cross." In the Colossians passage the law is viewed as an instrument of condemnation, a legal note of indebtedness for which we were liable but the demands of which we were unable to satisfy. Christ by his death paid our debt, canceled the bond, and took it forever out of the way. The imagery of the Colossians passage is different from that of its Ephesian parallel, and the application of its truth is somewhat different; but the main burden of the two passages is essentially the same.

Whether the law be viewed as a wall dividing race from race or as an instrument of condemnation, Christ has nullified it, taken it out of the way. By the removal of the Mosaic system the hostility between Jew and Gentile was destroyed, and the dividing wall that kept the races apart was laid low.

The divine purpose in abrogating the law is stated in verses 15–16. First, it was that Christ might "make in himself of twain [Jew and Gentile] one new man." This statement is an advance upon verse 14. It is not simply that the two races are made into one man, but into one *new* man. The thought is not merely that the two races are brought together, with the Jew remaining a Jew and the Gentile continuing as a Gentile. Nor is it that the Gentile becomes a Jew, nor that the Jew becomes a Gentile. The idea is of the creation out of the two of something entirely new—a new humanity, a new people of God.

This "new man" is created in Christ ("himself"). He lays one hand on the Jew, the other on the Gentile, and brings the two together in himself. So long as Jew and Gentile are unbelievers they continue to be at enmity with one another. It is only as each is united to Christ that they come to be at harmony one with the other.

The second purpose in the annulment of the law is expressed in verse 16—"that he might reconcile both [Jew and Gentile together] unto God in one body." Here the emphasis shifts from the relationship between Jew and Gentile to the relationship of both to God. Though brought in second in the passage, this concept is undoubtedly first in importance.

2. *Gentile and Jew at Peace with God* (vv. 16–18)

Christ not only unites Jew and Gentile into one new man; he also reconciles both to God. The two acts, though stated separately, are actually simultaneous. The union of the two hostile races is intimately bound up with, and indeed is based upon, the larger concept of reconciliation to God; for the death of enmity among men is conditioned upon the death of their enmity against God. The "one body" is not Christ's physical body but rather his mystical or spiritual body, of which believing Jews and believing Gentiles are both members. Christ desired to "bring the two long-sundered and antagonistic parties as one whole, one great body, into right relation to God by His cross." [6]

This is one of the four New Testament passages which treat the work of Christ under the figure of reconciliation. (The others are Rom. 5:10f; 2 Cor. 5:18ff; Col. 1:19ff.) The word "reconcile" suggests a change of relations between God and men and implies a previous state of estrangement and enmity. Note carefully that it is not God who is reconciled to man, but man who is reconciled to God. The New Testament always presents this point of view, for it is man's sin that has caused the enmity. The meaning is not, however, that Christ's reconciling activities are concerned only with man.

Reconciliation is not purely a subjective process. It was in some sense effected outside man before anything happened within him. This idea is implied in Paul's words in Romans 5:11, "through whom we have now received the reconciliation" (ASV). A reconciliation that can be received must in some sense be an accomplished fact before men receive it. In other words, reconciliation is both Godward and manward.

The death of Jesus removes the offending sin from man's heart and turns away the divine wrath. Man receives, or accepts, what God has wrought.

Christ by his death secured peace. He also preached the glad tidings of it "to you [Gentiles] which were afar off, and to them that were nigh [the Jews]" (v. 17). (Cf. Isa. 52:7; 57:19.) The peace mentioned is, of course, that which has been under discussion throughout this passage—peace between Jew and Gentile and peace between both and God. The question that arises from this statement is *when* and *how* this preaching was done. That the statement here cannot refer to Christ's personal ministry on earth is clear from two considerations. First, the preaching of peace to the Gentiles did not characterize his ministry on earth. Second, the context of verse 17 suggests that the preaching followed the accomplishing of reconciliation on the cross. We conclude, then, that the coming referred to (v. 17) was Christ's coming in the Spirit and the preaching was that done by Christ through his apostles and other believers.

Verse 18 affords proof that peace has been secured and announced for both Jews and Gentiles, "For through him we both [Jews and Gentiles] have access by one Spirit unto the Father." Every word is important. "For" shows the connection of the sentence with what has gone before. "Access," a word used by the ancients of the introduction of someone to a royal court, speaks here both of unhindered approach to God and of actual introduction into the divine presence (cf. Rom. 5:2). In the Old Testament economy only the high priest could enter into the holy of holies, and that only once each year. But in Christ all believers have continual access. "Both" emphasizes that this privilege is shared by Jew and Gentile alike. The prepositions in the sentence are very meaningful and deserving of careful observation. Our access is "through" Christ, "by" (better, "in") the Spirit, and "to" the Father. The doctrine of the Trinity, though not explicitly taught here, is obviously implied.

3. *Gentile and Jew Sharing the Privileges and Blessings of the Gospel* (vv. 19–22)

Verses 19–22 draw a number of inferences from the teaching which has been set forth in verses 13–18. These all have to do with the new fellowship into which believing Jews and believing Gentiles have been brought. The stress, however, is on the elevation of the Gentile to a position of equal privilege and benefit. Three figures are used to express this: a nation, a family, a building.

With regard to the first of these figures, Paul assures his Gentile readers that they are "no more strangers and foreigners, but fellowcitizens with the saints" (v. 19). They have been spiritually enfranchised. "Strangers and foreigners" was a comprehensive expression including all who for various reasons did not enjoy the full rights of citizenship in a city or nation. Once this status was the condition of the Gentiles in regard to the theocracy of Israel (cf. 2:11–12), but no longer is it so. "Saints" is a name for the people of God, the whole community of believers. In Christ national restrictions have been removed, and all Gentile believers are a part of the true "Israel of God" (Gal. 6:16). They share alike, with all who belong to it, the privileges and benefits of the new spiritual commonwealth.

The political figure gives way (v. 19) to a domestic one. Paul's readers are not only "fellowcitizens with the saints," they are also members "of the household [family] of God." This statement suggests that the fellowship of believers is of the closest, warmest kind. But beyond this idea, it speaks of the intimate relationship which all Christians sustain to God. They are his family and may address him as Father.

Verse 20 introduces the figure of a building. Believing Gentiles, along with believing Jews, are being built into a great spiritual structure "upon the foundation of the apostles and prophets, Jesus Christ himself being the chief corner stone."

How are we to understand "the foundation of the apostles and prophets"? Are the apostles and prophets themselves the foundation? Or does the statement mean that the foundation is laid by them? Paul in another place says, "Other foundation can no man lay than that is laid, which is Jesus Christ" (1 Cor. 3:11). However, since the relation of Christ to the building is in this passage expressed by another figure ("chief corner stone"), it is probably better to think of the foundation as *consisting* of the apostles and prophets. (The context suggests that these are New Testament prophets, of whom more will be said later [cf. 3:5; 4:11].) Christ is chief cornerstone; apostles and prophets are the foundation; other believers are the superstructure.

The cornerstone was the great stone put in the angle of the substructure where the walls met. It was the stone on which the stability of the whole building depended. Christ as chief cornerstone is thus the one who supports and holds together both the foundation and the walls. It is he who gives to this wondrous spiritual edifice its unity and its strength. Indeed, everything ultimately depends on him.

Paul adds that in union with Christ ("in whom"), "all the building" by being "fitly framed together" is growing (like a living organism) into a "holy temple [sanctuary] in the Lord" (v. 21). He reminds his readers of the part they have in this glorious structure. They (and believers of every age) who once were without hope and without God in the world are now being "builded together." The process is going on "through [by] the Spirit," to produce "a habitation of God" (v. 22). The entire building process has as its goal the perfecting of a great spiritual dwelling place for God (spoken of in v. 21 as a "temple," and in v. 22 as a "habitation").

Differences of opinion about these verses center largely in

the phrase "all the building" (v. 21). The King James Version suggests the picture of one great spiritual building which grows (both in compactness and in size) as each new believer is added to the structure (cf. 1 Peter 2:5). The imagery in the American Standard Version is that of a number of smaller buildings being joined together so as to form one whole structure. Some interpreters see an allusion to the many buildings and courts which made up the Jerusalem Temple. They understand Paul's words as referring to the many local congregations ("each several building") increasing in number and completeness so as to form together one great holy temple in the Lord.

ACTIVITIES FOR ENRICHMENT

Did you enjoy the activity with the hymnbook suggested for chapter 4? Examine the words of the hymn, "In Christ There Is No East or West," to find ideas based on Ephesians 2:11–22.

Consider the timeliness of these ideas as guidance in dealing with problems that are acute in our nation and in many parts of the world.

---

[1] F. F. Bruce, *The Epistle to the Ephesians* (New York: Fleming H. Revell Company, 1961), p. 54.

[2] James Denney, *The Death of Christ* (London: Hodder and Stoughton, 1907), p. 201.

[3] John Eadie, *Commentary on the Epistle to the Ephesians* (reprint ed.; Grand Rapids: Zondervan Publishing House, n.d.), p. 167.

[4] *Ibid.*, p. 170.

[5] *Ibid.*, p. 171.

[6] S. D. F. Salmond, *The Expositor's Greek Testament* (Grand Rapids: Wm. B. Eerdmans Publishing Company), III, 297.

CHAPTER 6

I. An Explanation of Paul's Special Ministry (3:2–13)
  1. The Nature of Paul's Ministry (vv. 2–7,13)
     (1) Stewardship (vv. 2–6)
     (2) Service (v. 7)
     (3) Suffering (v. 13)
  2. The Purpose of Paul's Ministry (vv. 8–13)
     (1) A missionary purpose (v. 8)
     (2) A theological purpose (v. 9)
     (3) An ultimate purpose (vv. 10–13)

II. A Prayer Occasioned by Contemplation of Paul's Ministry (3:1,14–21)
  1. The Approach to the Prayer (vv. 14–15)
  2. The Boldness of the Prayer (v. 16a)
  3. The Content of the Prayer (vv. 16b–19)
     (1) A request for inner power (vv. 16–17a)
     (2) A request for comprehension (vv. 17b–19a)
     (3) A request for the fulness of God (v. 19b)
  4. Paul's Confidence in God's Ability to Answer the Prayer (vv. 20–21)

6

Paul's Special Ministry in Regard to God's New People

Ephesians 3:1–21

THIS CHAPTER, the most intensely personal section of the Ephesian epistle, consists of a prayer (vv. 1,14–21) which is interrupted by a long digression (vv. 2–13). The digression, which forms an extended interpretation of Paul's special ministry to the Gentiles, is really the heart of the chapter. It is a sort of explanatory parenthesis which Paul felt was essential to the full appreciation of the prayer he had on his heart for his readers.

I. AN EXPLANATION OF PAUL'S SPECIAL MINISTRY (3:2–13)

Paul's mention of his appointed ministry to the Gentiles (v. 1) leads him to consider in greater detail its nature (vv. 2–7,13) and purpose (vv. 8–13). (Observe how in this chapter he repeatedly relates his work to the Gentiles, particularly in vv. 1,2,8,13.)

1. *The Nature of Paul's Ministry* (vv. 2–7,13)

Paul is confident that his readers have some awareness of his unique mission in the work of the gospel. Yet he feels it necessary to remind them of his ministry and to explain in some detail its significance. The various ideas expressed may be summed up under three words.

(1) *Stewardship (vv. 2–6).*—According to the reading of the King James Version, Paul describes his work as a "dis-

pensation of the grace of God which is given me to you-ward"
(v. 2). The word "dispensation" denotes an arrangement or a
plan; it says nothing specifically about the nature of Paul's
work, but rather points up the mode in which he had been
selected for it. That is, it was not of his own choosing but was
the result of an arrangement or administration by which the
grace of God was given to him. But the Greek word translated "dispensation" was employed in New Testament times
of the office and function of the trusted steward of a household (cf. Luke 16:2–4). It is best rendered by our word
"stewardship." Paul's use of it here shows that he conceived
of his position as both a high privilege and a sacred trust. (Cf.
1 Cor. 9:17; Col. 1:25; 1 Peter 4:10.)

Three things are said about this stewardship. First, it concerned the "grace of God" (v. 2). The word "grace" as used
here is a comprehensive term summing up the whole of Paul's
spiritual privilege. To speak of a stewardship of this grace
is to acknowledge that God's favor is given not to be enjoyed
as a private luxury but to be shared with others.

Second, Paul's stewardship of grace had particular reference to his Gentile readers ("to you-ward," v. 2). God's house
(2:20–22) is composed of the redeemed from various racial
groups, but Paul felt it was his special function to build the
Gentile portion of that house.

Third, this stewardship involved a great "mystery" of redemption. We have seen that a mystery in the New Testament
is something previously concealed but now made known in
the gospel. In 1:9 "mystery" spoke of God's purpose of gathering together all things under the headship of Christ. Here
it refers to one phase of that ultimate goal, namely, the in-
clusion of Gentiles in the blessings of the gospel and the terms
on which this is done.

Verses 3–5 explain Paul's understanding of the mystery. It
came not through the instructions of others but by an immediate revelation from God. Enough had been written (cf. 1:9–

11; 2 : 11–22) to show that Paul had special knowledge of this mystery and therefore special authority to speak of it.

Verse 5 expressly says that in past generations this divine secret was "not made known unto the sons of men, as it is now revealed unto his holy apostles and prophets by the Spirit." The stress falls on the word "as," the thought being that the mystery had not been made known with the fulness and clarity that now it has. That Gentiles were included in God's purpose was, in a way, known in Old Testament times. Even to Abraham it was said, "In thee shall all families of the earth be blessed" (Gen. 12 : 3). "But what was not fore-seen in Old Testament times was the fact that these promised gospel-blessings would involve the creation of 'one new man' (Eph. 2. 15) by the incorporation of Jewish and Gentile be-lievers alike, on the common ground of divine grace." [1]

It is just this point that Paul stresses in verse 6, where he gives the content of the mystery of Christ: "that the Gentiles are fellow-heirs and fellow-members of the body, and fellow-partakers of the promise in Christ Jesus through the gospel" (ASV). Note the repetition of the term "fellow." Its reiteration is the key to the meaning and significance of the verse. Gen-tiles are not second-class citizens in God's kingdom; they are admitted to its blessings as equals. They are "fellow-heirs" in relation to Jewish believers, "fellow-members" in relation to the body of Christ, and "fellow-partakers" in relation to the historic promises of God.

(2) Service (v. 7).—In verses 2–6 we have seen how God revealed the secret that Gentiles are included equally with Jews in his purpose of grace. Paul interpreted his relation to this purpose in terms of stewardship. The apostle moves one step beyond this idea in verse 7. Here he declares that God had made him a "minister" of the good news of salvation by which the Gentiles were actually to be brought in. That is to say, Paul's stewardship was carried out in the service of the gospel. The Greek word for "minister," meaning servant

or attendant, is the word from which we get our word "deacon." Here it denotes one who serves in the interest of, and for the benefit of another. The word itself is used in the New Testament in reference to the apostles and their helpers (for example, 2 Cor. 6:4; 1 Tim. 4:6). It is used of Christ (Rom. 15:8). It is even used of the servants of Satan (2 Cor. 11:15). Christ used the verb form when he said, "I am among you as he that serveth" (Luke 22:27) and, "For even the Son of man came not to be ministered unto, but to minister" (Mark 10:45).

When Paul says he was "made" a minister he indicates that he did not take this honor to himself; he was divinely appointed to his office. He looked upon this appointment in two ways. First, it was a great favor. He was not made a minister in consideration of any worthiness or merit within himself, but rather "according to the gift of [consisting in] the grace of God" (v. 7). Second, Paul saw his introduction into the ministry as involving the exercise of divine power. He was made a minister "by [according to, in proportion to] the effectual working of his [God's] power" (v. 7). Paul never ceased to wonder that one such as he, once fanatically devoted to Judaism, should be apostle to the Gentiles. His apostleship was to him nothing less than the result of the working of the omnipotence of God. His words recall the scene on the Damascus road, with its blazing light outshining the noonday sun. Here, to be sure, was grace unspeakable, but here also was limitless power.

(3) *Suffering* (*v. 13*).—Paul not only saw his work as a stewardship of grace and as a service in the gospel by which the Gentiles were being brought into God's redemptive purpose; he also interpreted it in terms of suffering. He knew from experience that the way of service is not always an easy way. For him the calling of God meant blood, sweat, and tears. Read the catalog of his trials in 2 Corinthians 11:23–28. Indeed, even as he wrote this letter there dangled from his

wrist a chain which bound him twenty-four hours a day to a Roman soldier.

The word translated "tribulations" literally means "pressure" but is used generally in the Bible in the sense of affliction or tribulation. Paul's afflictions, he tells his Gentile readers, are "for you" (v. 13). The sufferings were incurred in their interest, in the carrying out of his mission in their behalf (cf. Col. 1:24).

2. *The Purpose of Paul's Ministry* (vv. 8–13)

Paul magnified the dignity of his office, but he was always possessed with a sense of his own personal unworthiness. "Unto me [the pronoun is emphatic], who am less than the least of all saints, is this grace given" (v. 8).

The Greek word rendered "less than the least" is a most unusual one, found only in this passage. It is really a superlative form to which Paul added a comparative ending; "leaster," if there were such a word, would be the meaning. It was not enough for Paul to use a word that meant "least"; he wanted a place beneath the least. One thinks of the old Puritan who said, "I do not quarrel with Paul's language, but I do dispute his right to push me out of my place. Less than the least," said he, "is my place."

The "grace" (v. 8) refers to Paul's office, his apostleship. Having called attention to it, he proceeds to state a threefold purpose God had in calling him to this office.

(1) *A missionary purpose* (v. 8).—God's intention was that Paul "should preach among the Gentiles the unsearchable riches of Christ." The entire statement is deeply meaningful. In the Greek "Gentiles" is emphatic by its position. It was Paul's unique ministry in relation to them that still occupied his mind and filled his heart with wonder. To him it was a high and thrilling privilege to proclaim that the Messiah promised to the Jews is Saviour of the Gentiles also. From the word for "preach," which means "to announce glad tidings,"

our word "evangelize" is derived. Most suggestive is Paul's description of his message as "the unsearchable riches of Christ." The phrase brings to mind the boundless resources in Christ for meeting the needs of sinful humanity. These resources, Paul declares, are "unsearchable." This vivid word, meaning literally "untrackable" or "inexplorable," denotes that which is too vast to be measured.

It suggests the figure of a man standing, with uplifted hands, in a posture of great amazement, before continuous revelations of immeasurable and unspeakable glory. . . . It is as if a man were tracking out the confines of a lake, walking its boundaries, and when the circuit were almost complete should discover that it was no lake at all, but an arm of the ocean, and that he was confronted by the immeasurable sea! [2]

The word is found elsewhere in the New Testament only in Romans 11:33. There it is used of the ways and purposes of God and suggests that which is unfathomable, beyond human comprehension.

(2) A *theological purpose* (*v.* 9).—A second purpose of Paul's ministry was "to make all men see what is the fellowship of the mystery." In these words Paul depicts himself as a teacher whose task it is to bring out the profound implications of the gospel. God particularly wanted him to cause all men to see the scope of the divine plan of redemption.

Actually, this clause is very closely related to the one just discussed, for it was by preaching to the Gentiles the unsearchable riches of Christ that the mystery of redemption was made manifest to the world. Preaching the gospel to the Gentiles, says Lenski, "was like setting the deep mystery into the fullest light of day so that all men might see it." [3]

In verse 9 the word for "fellowship" (King James Version) is better translated "dispensation" or "stewardship" (as in 3:2). The thought concerns the worldwide distribution of the news and blessings of the gospel and the manner in which God intends this to be done. The chief thing, however, concerns Paul's relation to all this. God's intention had always been to offer a redemption of worldwide application, but for all practical purposes that intention lay unrevealed in his own bosom until in the gospel it was made an open secret. The stewardship (or administration) of the secret, the particular manner in which God would convey and apply it to the world at large, was for Paul to make known.

(3) *An ultimate purpose* (*vv. 10–13*).—Most of us, even from the vantage point of the twentieth century, have a very limited concept of the breadth, the grandeur, the infinite range of God's purpose of grace. Something of the magnitude and completeness of that purpose is suggested by verses 10–11. Here Paul states the ultimate aim of his preaching the gospel to the Gentiles and of his enlightening all men regarding the stewardship of a world-embracing redemption. It is all "to the intent that now unto the principalities and powers in heavenly places might be known by the church the manifold wisdom of God" (v. 10). Notice that the recipients of this new knowledge are "the principalities and powers in heavenly places." That angelic beings are intensely interested in human redemption is clear from 1 Peter 1:12. Here we are told that their knowledge and blessedness are increased by the exhibition of the work of God in the salvation of men.

Again, observe that what they learn concerns not the love or power of God but "the manifold wisdom of God." Peter writes of God's "manifold grace" (1 Peter 4:10), but the adjective he uses is not exactly the same as the one employed here. Paul's word for "manifold," found only here in the New Testament, is an especially vivid one, literally meaning "many colored." It may make allusion to the intricate beauty of an embroidered pattern. Probably the main idea in this text is that of infinite beauty and diversity. This beauty of God's wisdom is to be demonstrated by and through the church.

It seems that the wisdom of God is especially mentioned in reference to the complicated problem of human redemp-

tion and, more particularly, the plan for the proclamation of
that redemption on a worldwide scale. Eadie eloquently
states that angelic beings

have seen much of God's working—many a sun lighted up, and
many a world launched into its orbit. They have been delighted
with the solution of many a problem, and the development of
many a mystery. But in the proclamation of the gospel to the
Gentiles, . . . involving the origination and extinction of Judaism,
the incarnation and the atonement, the manger and the cross . . .
"these principalities and powers in heavenly places" beheld with
rapture other and brighter phases of a wisdom which had often
dazzled them by its brilliant and profuse versatility.[4]

The special instrument of instruction to these heavenly
beings is "the church," referred to here in its broadest significance as made up of the whole body of redeemed people. The
chief point is that the very existence of the church, uniting
hostile sections of mankind in one body, is an obvious proof
that God is gathering up all creation in Christ. The church is
thus viewed as the visible materialization of the purpose of
God for the universe.

In verse 12 Paul adds that through our union with Christ
"we have boldness and access with confidence by the faith
of [i.e., through faith in] him." Note the three leading words:
"boldness," "access," "confidence." All this we have in Christ.
"Boldness," suggesting absence of restraint or fear, translates
a Greek word which literally denotes freedom of speech. It
was used in classical Greek of the free speech which was the
right of every citizen of a democratic state. In the New Testament it signifies the liberty of believers to approach God directly through Christ, with the added notion of freedom from
fear of being rejected. "Access," which betokens approach to
God (cf. 2:18) is the principal word here. "Confidence" suggests assurance of acceptance. The three words are bound together so as to form one complete idea, namely, that through
faith in Christ we have free, unrestricted, confident access to
God.

The long parenthesis begun at verse 2 is concluded in verse 13. "Wherefore" seems to refer back to the entire exposition of God's purpose and Paul's involvement in it (vv. 2–12). He did not want his readers to lose heart concerning the great cause of Gentile evangelization. His imprisonment did not mean that the word of God was bound nor that God's purpose was frustrated. Nor did his afflictions mean that he was out of the path of duty. Indeed, his sufferings were the direct consequence of his obedience to, and participation in, the eternal purpose of God for the redemption of the race. The readers, instead of being discouraged at Paul's afflictions, should glory in them, for they were an evidence that God's purpose of grace was advancing toward its consummation.

Before proceeding to consider the remainder of this chapter, one would do well to ponder some of the concepts and impressions conveyed by the first thirteen verses. Look carefully at the heart of Paul as it is laid bare in the passage—his consciousness of divine appointment, his sense of personal unworthiness, his appreciation of the greatness of his work, and his sense of wonder at the message of redemption. Again, consider the marvelous scope of God's redemptive purpose, the unique task which God's people have in relation to that purpose, and how full and wonderful is the gospel of grace.

II. A PRAYER OCCASIONED BY CONTEMPLATION OF PAUL'S MINISTRY (3:1,14–21)

Following the parenthesis in verses 2–13, Paul gets back to his prayer, begun in verse 1.

1. The Approach to the Prayer (vv. 14–15)

"For this cause" (v. 14), suggests the reason for the prayer and resumes the line of thought interrupted by the parenthesis of verses 2–13. It points in a general way to the teaching of 2:11–22 concerning all that God had wrought in Christ for the Gentile. More particularly, it refers to those aspects of

the divine purpose set forth in 3 : 2–13. Paul's prayer, therefore, was offered because of his deep interest in the people of
God, because of his sincere desire that his Gentile readers
might enter fully into their privileges in Christ.

The customary posture in prayer among the Jews was that
of standing (cf. Mark 11 : 25; Luke 18 : 11, 13); a kneeling position betokened special solemnity or unusual urgency (cf.
Luke 22 : 41; Acts 7 : 60). With us it is much the same. Sometimes one may close his eyes and lift his heart in prayer to
God while sitting quietly in a favorite chair. Sometimes, as in
our services of public worship, we may engage in prayer while
standing. But there are other times when there is such intense
earnestness, such an overwhelming burden, that one finds
himself irresistibly forced to his knees. Therefore, when Paul
says, "I bow my knees," the words are indicative of the intense
earnestness and the unusual emotion which he felt.

The prayer is addressed to "the Father of our Lord Jesus
Christ, of whom the whole family in heaven and earth is
named" (vv. 14–15). The words translated by "of our Lord
Jesus Christ" are not in the best manuscripts and are accordingly omitted from modern translations. Paul is thinking not
so much of God's relation to Christ as of his relation to his
redeemed people.

The translation in the King James Version, "the whole
family," refers to the company of the redeemed, both in
heaven and upon earth, as making up one great family with
God as Father. Interpreters who translate the expression
"every family" understand Paul to mean that every group of
intelligent beings, whether in heaven or on earth, gets the
name "family" from the one Father.

The descriptive clause, "of whom the whole family . . . is
named," is most remarkable. There is a play on words in the
Greek that unfortunately cannot be adequately expressed in
an English translation, for the Greek word for "family"
(*patria*) is built on the same root as the word for "father"

(*pater*). The thought may be partly expressed thus: "I bow my knees to the Father from whom all fatherhood is named" (i.e., derives its name and nature).

The fatherhood of God is not merely a metaphor drawn from human relationships. The converse is true. He is the fountain of fatherhood and all fatherliness. The original, archetypal fatherhood is God's; all others are in some sense derived from him. The human relationship is only a reflection of which the divine fatherhood is the reality. Well does Bruce say that "the more nearly any fatherhood, natural or spiritual, approaches in character to God's perfect Fatherhood, the more truly does it manifest fatherhood as God intended it to be." [5]

2. *The Boldness of the Prayer* (v. 16a)

The opening of verse 16 suggests the great boldness of Paul in prayer (cf. 3:12). In the requests which he makes of God his desire is that God may grant them "according to [on the pattern of] the riches of his glory." Paul had in mind the infinite perfections of God, and he is asking that in accordance with this his readers may receive the benefits they require. Sometimes we seem to be fearful lest we should ask too much of God. We approach him timidly, as though we were not sure he could meet our needs. Let us learn from Paul's inspired prayer that we can never strain the resources of God. He does not give grudgingly nor in meager portions, as if he were afraid he might exhaust his wealth. He gives according to the measure of his infinite fulness.

3. *The Content of the Prayer* (vv. 16b-19)

There are three petitions in Paul's prayer, each introduced in the Greek text by the same conjunction (*hina*). But they are progressive rather than co-ordinate. Closely knit, with thought melting into thought, they "open out one into the other like some majestic suite of apartments in a great palace-temple, each leading into a loftier and more spacious hall, each drawing nearer the presence-chamber, until at last we stand there." [6] The climax of the prayer is "that ye might be filled with all the fulness of God" (v. 19).

(1) *A request for inner power* (vv. 16–17a).—The first request, for inner power, is contained in the words, "That he would grant you . . . to be strengthened with might by his Spirit in the inner man; [so] that Christ may dwell in your hearts by faith." This power is divine in kind, communicated by the Spirit, and realized in "the inner man," i.e., in the seat of intellectual and spiritual life.

The issue and result of such divine strengthening is the indwelling of Christ. However, Paul is not referring to the coming of Christ into the heart at conversion. The persons in behalf of whom this supplication was originally made were already believers and in a true sense indwelt by the living Christ. What Paul desired was that Christ's presence in them might be both real and regnant. Graham Scroggie explains that Christ's

presence in us has its degrees and advances, its less and more, its outer and inner. A life may be truly Christian and yet far from fully Christian. It is this which distinguishes one Christian from another. Some have made little room for Christ, some give Him more, and in some He has the whole house. Or, viewed from another standpoint, in some Christ is just present, in others He is prominent, and in others again, He is pre-eminent.[7]

(2) *A request for comprehension* (vv. 17b–19a).—The second petition, "that ye . . . may be able to comprehend . . . and to know the love of Christ," grows out of the first. In a general sense it is a prayer that believers, as a consequence of the divine strengthening and indwelling, may have spiritual capacity for understanding the love of Christ. There are two conditions of knowing this love. One is that we ourselves be "rooted [securely settled] and grounded [deeply founded].

in love" (v. 17). The other is that we be endowed with super-natural power (v. 18).

The thought of the petition revolves around two phrases: "to comprehend" (v. 18) and "to know" (v. 19). The first betokens a mental grasp and might better be rendered by the word "apprehend." The idea is of laying hold on something so as to make it one's own. The object which we are to apprehend is not specifically stated; only the dimensions of it are given—"the breadth, and length, and depth, and height." Most interpreters think the object of comprehension is "the love of Christ" (v. 19). The mention of dimensions is rhetorical, setting forth in a striking manner the surpassing magnitude of God's love. To say that it "passeth knowledge" means that we can never hope to have an absolute and complete understanding of it.

But we are not only to apprehend this love; we are also "to know" it. The word for "know" denotes knowledge gained by experience and may be somewhat stronger in force than "apprehend."

One should not overlook the phrase, "with all saints." No one of us will ever be able to take in all the love of God, but each can comprehend a little, and together we may explore its measureless reaches.

> For the love of God is broader
> Than the measure of man's mind;
> And the heart of the Eternal
> Is most wonderfully kind.
>
> FREDERICK W. FABER

(3) *A request for the fulness of God* (v. 19b). The final issue of all that Paul prays for is "that ye might be filled with [up to the measure of] all the fulness of God." In this filling every other blessing is included. The "fulness of God" seems to be an expression standing for the sum total of all the energies, powers, and attributes of God. Of course, Paul does not mean to suggest that mortal men can ever contain within

themselves the fulness of the divine essence, and we must guard against so interpreting his words. Solomon long before had declared that "heaven and the heaven of heavens cannot contain" God (2 Chron. 6:18). What then is the import of Paul's words? His prayer is that his readers may experience the totality of blessings which God is willing and able to bestow. But more specifically, it is that their whole being may be filled with God's presence and power, so that there shall be no room for more—like the teacup on the seashore filled to overflowing with the swelling water of the vast ocean.

This petition staggers the imagination, but we must not set it aside as an impossibility. Indeed, every believer already knows something of this experience, for "of his fulness have all we received, and grace for grace" (John 1:16). And in another part of this epistle Paul sets before us the goal of growing "unto the measure of the stature of the fulness of Christ" (Eph. 4:13). In light of this overwhelming idea, Maclaren fittingly reminds us that "Paul's prayers are God's promises; and we are justified in taking these rapturous petitions as being distinct declarations of God's desire and purpose for each of us." [8]

(A number of interpreters feel that the "ye" (vv. 17,19) is collective. They understand Paul to be pleading for something that pertains to the whole body of Christ, not Christians as individuals.)

Scroggie sums up the three petitions in this manner:

By the strengthening of the Spirit Christ will come to dwell more largely and richly in our hearts, and this double blessing will result in a fuller apprehension and knowledge of the love of God in Christ, and all this will have for its issue our being ever more completely "filled into the fulness of God." [9]

4. Paul's Confidence in God's Ability to Answer the Prayer (vv. 20–21)

Paul's confidence is expressed in the form of a lofty doxol-

ogy. Whatever our requests may be, we can never exceed
God's ability to answer. He is able to do "superabundantly"
more than we ask, more even than our imagination can conceive. This he does "according to the power that worketh in
us" (v. 20). We have learned already in this epistle that the
power at work in us is none other than the power of God that
raised Christ from the dead and quickened us from spiritual
death (1:19ff).

The chapter closes with a reference to the church as the
sphere within which the glory of God is exhibited, the suggestion being that the glory of God is the end for which the
church exists.

ACTIVITIES FOR ENRICHMENT

Reread Ephesians 3:1–21 in several translations. Point out the
missionary implications in this passage. Consider its teaching about
the obligations of believers in any age.

Meditate on God's plan for using his redeemed people, the
church which is the body of Christ, as a demonstration of his
wisdom and purpose (3:10–11). Silently ask: Is my life a good
demonstration of the purpose God had in mind in saving me?

---

[1] F. F. Bruce, *The Epistle to the Ephesians* (New York: Fleming H.
Revell Company, 1961), p. 61.

[2] John Henry Jowett, *The Passion for Souls* (New York: Fleming H.
Revell Company, 1905), pp. 9–10.

[3] R. C. H. Lenski, *The Interpretation of St. Paul's Epistles to the Galatians, to the Ephesians, and to the Philippians* (Columbus, Ohio: The
Wartburg Press, 1946), pp. 477–78. Reprinted by permission of Augs-
burg Publishing House, copyright owners by assignment from the Wartburg Press.

[4] John Eadie, *Commentary on the Epistle to the Ephesians* (reprint
ed.; Grand Rapids: Zondervan Publishing House, n.d.), p. 234.

[5] Bruce, *op. cit.*, p. 67.

[6] Alexander Maclaren, *Expositions of Holy Scripture* (Grand Rapids:
Wm. B. Eerdmans Publishing Company, 1942), XVI, 132.

[7] W. Graham Scroggie, *Paul's Prison Prayers* (London: Pickering and
Inglis Ltd., n.d.), p. 70.

[8] *Op. cit.*, p. 172.

[9] *Op. cit.*, pp. 77–78.

CHAPTER 7

The Daily Walk of God's New People:
Spiritual Obligations

Ephesians 4:1–16

To FACILITATE our study of Ephesians we have broken up the text into nine sections. The epistle may be seen, however, as composed of only two major divisions. One is distinctly doctrinal (chaps. 1–3), and the other is mainly practical or hortatory (chaps. 4–6). The pivotal verse of the whole epistle —indeed, the key that unlocks its structure—may be said to be Ephesians 4:1. It gathers up in a single phrase ("the vocation wherewith ye are called") the theme of chapters 1–3. In a succinct appeal ("walk worthy") it announces the emphasis of chapters 4–6. The inference is that the high calling which the Christian has experienced carries with it very weighty responsibilities.

I. To Walk as Becomes a Christian (4:1)

"Walk" is a word used in the Scriptures to define the course of one's life. In Genesis, for example, Enoch is said to have "walked with God." And John reminds us of our obligation as Christians to walk even as Jesus walked (1 John 2:6). To "walk worthy of the vocation wherewith ye are called" means to live in a way that is in harmony with that holy calling. In the present passage the appeal for worthy living contains a general principle designed to guide the whole of life. Detailed applications of the principle follow in the remainder of the epistle.

Verses 2–16 emphasize the *spiritual* qualities which are becoming to the life of those who have been called to be God's people. Paul mentions particularly those things which are essential to right relationships within the community of the redeemed, the things that enhance the fellowship and the over-all well-being of the body of Christ. Just as it is of primary importance that a child learn to get along with members of his own family, so believers must first learn to relate themselves properly and worthily to other members of God's redeemed family.

II. To Promote the Unity of the Spirit (4:2–6)

One thing essential to a worthy Christian life is an earnest effort to promote "the unity of the Spirit."

1. *The Admonition to Unity* (vv. 2–3)

Verse 1 has spoken of walking worthily of the Christian calling. The language there is general enough to include the whole of Christian conduct. Verses 2–3, however, narrow the range to one area of the Christian life—the relationship of believers to one another. Some four or five items are mentioned in these verses, but they must be seen as constituting one unit admonition reaching its climax in the words, "endeavouring to keep the unity of the Spirit in the bond of peace" (v. 3).

(1) *The nature of the unity desired.*—The context suggests that the unity Paul had in mind is not external ecclesiastical union. It is a heart unity and concerns relationships and attitudes rather than organization (cf. Phil. 2:2). The word translated "unity" is an abstract term for what is elsewhere in the Scriptures referred to as "fellowship."

(2) *Our responsibility in regard to unity.*—The production of true unity among God's people is the work of the Spirit. It cannot be legislated into being, nor can it be brought about

by the mechanics of organization. This fact does not mean, however, that we are to do nothing to foster and nurture it.

First, we are to endeavor to *keep* "the unity of the Spirit" (v. 3). The unity already exists as a spiritual reality; it is our responsibility to keep it intact. "Endeavouring" suggests the inward effort that is required in maintaining this unity. For the Greek word translated "endeavouring" we have no precise equivalent in our language. It combines the ideas of haste, eagerness, and zeal. In several passages it is translated "give diligence." (See ASV, 2 Tim. 2:15; 4:21; 2 Peter 1:10; Heb. 4:11.)

Second, we are to practice those basic Christian virtues which help to conserve this unity. These are listed in verse 2: "lowliness" (humility), "meekness" (a word conveying the ideas of gentleness toward men and submission to God's will), "longsuffering" (the opposite of being short-tempered), and loving forbearance. The failure to cultivate and practice these graces has been at the root of many a church squabble and has generally been most destructive of the spiritual health of the churches.

2. *The Grounds of Unity* (vv. 4–6)

Verses 4–6 point to seven unities which constitute the foundation on which the Spirit effects a true oneness among the saints.

These seven unities fall into three groups. The first is "one body . . . one Spirit . . . one hope of your calling" (v. 4). The "one body" obviously refers to the church, which as comprised of all God's people is the body of Christ (cf. 1:23; 2:16). What is said of the church in this broad sense is in the main true of it also in its local manifestations (the churches), but the local concept is not primary here. The church through which "the manifold wisdom of God" is to be made known to "the principalities and powers in heavenly places" (3:10) is seen as one living organism. And just as there is one body, so also there is "one Spirit" who gives life to that body (cf. 1 Cor. 12:13). Finally, the common goal toward which all who belong to the body are progressing is the "one hope" of sharing ultimately in the glory of God (cf. Rom. 5:2; 1 John 3:2).

Second, there is "one Lord, one faith, one baptism" (v. 5). The first triad of unities centered in the third Person of the Trinity; this centers in the "one Lord," who is, of course, Jesus Christ. No one can rightly call himself Christian who does not acknowledge Christ in this manner (cf. Rom. 10:9). Early Christians jealously guarded this prerogative of the Saviour, and many of them died rather than invoke the Roman emperor as "lord." One of the best known of such instances is that of Polycarp, the aged bishop of Smyrna who lived in the second Christian century. When commanded to say, "Caesar is lord," he refused and made the noble confession: "Eighty-six years I have served him, and he has done me no wrong; how then can I blaspheme my Saviour and King?" Upon this word the faithful witness was sent to the stake to seal his testimony with his blood.

"Faith" is not to be taken objectively for a system of Christian doctrine. It is not a creed but the experience of faith or trust in the one Lord.

The "one baptism" is taken by some as a reference to Spirit-baptism, but it seems better to understand it as a reference to water baptism. The point of this verse is that there is one Lord who is to be obeyed and adored; one believing experience which brings people into saving union with that Lord; and one outward, visible ceremony by which believers confess their faith and are openly incorporated into the fellowship of God's people.

This glorious list of spiritual unities is climaxed and crowned by the statement that there is "one God and Father of all" (v. 6; cf. 1 Cor. 8:6). The one sovereign God is the ultimate source of spiritual unity. There is a sense, of course, in which God as Creator is "Father of all" (cf. Mal. 2:10), but the present context favors the limitation of the concept here to his being Father of all who are Christians. Jewish and Gentile believers, forming one redeemed body, have one God and Father. This one God is "above all, and through all, and in you all" (v. 6). (The "all" is general and unqualified, though the primary reference must still be to believers.)

The first phrase speaks of God's unshared sovereignty. He has, and can have, no superior. His throne, lifted high over all creation, is paramount and unchallenged. The second phrase speaks of God's immanence, his presence as pervading, controlling, and sustaining all things. Although he is over all, he does not live in remote indifference. His influence and power are everywhere felt. The third phrase, "in you all," speaks of God's indwelling and suggests a personal and intimate relationship. The one God and Father dwells "in" his people by his Spirit.

III. To Contribute to the Growth of the Church (4:7–16)

Believers are intended to perform two kinds of ministry. One is a missionary ministry to the world; they are to make disciples of all the nations. The other is an edifying ministry within the body of Christ. Each member is to do his part in the building up of that body until it attains "the measure of the stature of the fulness of Christ." The present passage constitutes a very important discussion of this latter responsibility.

1. Divine Provision for Growth (vv. 7–12)

God has provided for the growth of his church through the bestowal of manifold gifts upon his believing people. These gifts are not to be identified completely with natural endowments; they are to be understood mainly as special capacities for service granted to those who are in Christ (cf. Rom. 12:3–8; 1 Cor. 12:1–31).

Several matters of considerable importance are herein taught concerning spiritual gifts:

First, every Christian has a gift of some kind. A gift of "grace" is said to be "unto every one of us" (v. 7). To be sure, not everyone possesses a gift that places him conspicuously before the congregation, but each has a capacity for service somewhere within the body of Christ. And whether others consider it important or not, God deems it so. What a rebuke this truth is to those who imagine that there is nothing they can do in the church!

Second, there is wide diversity in these gifts. Saving grace is the same for all, but each believer's endowment for service is different. This fact is especially pointed up in verse 7. The word "but" marks a change of emphasis. Whereas the stress of verses 1–6 has been on the unity of the whole body of Christ, now the thought turns to the diversity of the individual parts that make up the whole. Each Christian possesses an individuality that God recognizes and uses in his service.

Third, the special grace which each Christian possesses is bestowed "according to the measure of the gift of Christ" (v. 7). The exalted Lord is sovereign in the distribution of gifts. "The rule is not our merit, nor our previous capacity, nor our asking, but his own good pleasure." [1] The logical inference arising from this truth is that each believer should be content with his gift, neither envying those whose gifts are more conspicuous and honorable in the eyes of men, nor looking down on those which seem less so than his own.

Fourth, the bestowal of these gifts is in accordance with a prophetic declaration concerning the ascended Messiah. Alluding to Psalm 68:18, Paul writes: "Wherefore he [God] saith, When he ascended up on high, he led captivity captive, and gave gifts unto men" (v. 8). The imagery is that of a military conqueror leading captives in triumph and laden with spoils, which he distributes to his followers. In the original context of the psalm it is God who is envisioned as the conqueror, but Paul sees a Messianic significance in the words. Thinking of the victory that was achieved at the cross, he applies them to the ascended Christ. Paul thinks of Christ as a conqueror enriched by his victories and giving gifts to his people.

Verses 9–10 are inserted parenthetically to explain verse 8 and to show that the passage quoted refers to Christ. *The New English Bible* accurately and clearly brings out the thought: "Now, the word 'ascended' implies that he also descended to the lowest level, down to the very earth. He who descended is no other than he who ascended far above all heavens, so that he might fill the universe."[2] Paul is saying that the ascension of such a divine person as is described by the psalmist necessarily implies a previous descent by that person from his heavenly abode. Christ is the one who thus descended; it must therefore have been he who was spoken of in the psalm as ascending.

The phrase "lower parts of the earth" (v. 9) may mean parts lower than the earth. Starting from this idea, some interpreters conclude that Christ descended into hell, the place of punishment. But it is seriously doubted that the Scriptures give any warrant to the idea of Christ's going into hell. A variant of this view takes the reference to be to Christ's descent into Hades, the realm of the dead (cf. Acts 2:25–35; Rom. 10:6). This interpretation is theologically sound and grammatically legitimate. Still another way of looking at this phrase, however, is to understand the Greek word for "earth" as a genitive of identity. The meaning then is "the parts lower [than heaven]; that is, the earth," the reference then being to the incarnation of Christ. Either of the last two interpretations yields a good meaning, but the last is to be preferred.

In verse 11 we learn that Christ not only bestows gifts upon men; the men so gifted are in turn bestowed upon the church to serve it in various ways. Some of these "gifts" are enumerated: Some are given to serve as apostles, some as prophets, some as evangelists, and others as pastors and teachers. The point is not that some men received the gift of apostleship, others prophecy, and so on. Rather, the persons thus endowed are themselves the gifts of the ascended Christ to the whole body of Christ. The men who fill the office, no less than the office itself, are gifts to the church.

"Apostles" and "prophets" (cf. 2:20; 3:5) appear to have been confined to the first Christian generation. Apostles, in the stricter use of the word, were those who had seen Christ (1 Cor. 9:1-2), were witnesses of his resurrection (Acts 1:8,21-23), and were immediately commissioned by him to preach (Matt. 10:5; Gal. 1:1). In a broader sense the word was used of those who, though not commissioned directly by Christ as were Paul and the Jerusalem apostles, preached the gospel in close association with such men. Thus Barnabas is called an apostle (Acts 14:4,14), and Timothy and Silas may be included in the word in 1 Thessalonians 2:6. "Prophets" performed a preaching function; they spoke under the immediate inspiration of the Spirit of God (cf. Acts 11:27ff; 13:1ff; 21:4,9; 1 Cor. 14:1ff). Through them, when there was as yet no New Testament, God gave guidance and direction to his people.

After the writings of the New Testament came into general circulation, the offices of apostle and prophet appear to have been withdrawn; but since evangelists and pastor-teachers are required by every generation, these offices continue. The Greek word for "evangelist" occurs only three times in the New Testament—once of Philip (Acts 21:8), once of Timothy (2 Tim. 4:5), and here. It speaks of one who announces glad tidings, one called and devoted to the direct proclamation of the good news of salvation. We may think of evangelists in

New Testament days as missionaries to the unconverted, as itinerant preachers endowed with clear perceptions of saving truth and possessed of unusual power in recommending it to others.

"Pastors and teachers" constitute one office with a dual function. (Observe the wording: "some, pastors and teachers," not "some pastors and some teachers.") The two functions coincide and are combined in one person. As suggested by the terms, a person occupying this office was both to shepherd (which is the idea in the word "pastor") the flock of God and to instruct them in divine truth. We may think of him as performing a settled ministry rather than itinerant. This is the only place in the New Testament where "pastor" is used of the office we know by that name. Elsewhere those who fill this office are called "bishops" or "overseers" (Acts 20:28; 1 Tim. 3:2) and "elders" (Acts 20:17; 1 Peter 5:1).

Christ's gift of apostles, prophets, evangelists, and pastor-teachers is for a specific purpose: "for the perfecting of the saints, for the work of the ministry, for the edifying of the body of Christ" (v. 12). The significance of this verse is obscured by the rendering of the King James Version. We may translate the idea: "with a view to the equipping [complete outfitting] of the saints for a work of service, [and this] for the building up of the body of Christ." The idea is that the "work of service" is done by the saints. It is the task of apostles, prophets, evangelists, and pastor-teachers to equip them for this service. This meaning fits in well with the statement (v. 7) that each believer has received a gift of grace, a capacity for service. Apostles, prophets, and all who have been given places of leadership in the church are the means provided for equipping the saints to render this service.

And what is the work of serving to achieve? The answer is in the final phrase of verse 12: "the edifying [building up] of the body of Christ." Toward this end every believer has a contribution to make.

2. *Ultimate Goal of Growth* (vv. 13–16)

Verses 13–16 explain what Paul had in mind when he spoke of the building up of the body of Christ—not numerical growth, but the attainment of spiritual maturity.

(1) *The goal defined* (*v. 13*).—Verse 13 gives a general statement concerning the goal of growth: "Till we all [the whole number of us] come in [arrive at] the unity of the faith, and of the knowledge of the Son of God, unto a perfect man, unto the measure of the stature of the fulness of Christ." The pivotal words are the conjunction "till," the verb "come," and the prepositions "in" and "unto." The "till" indicates the period during which the ministries mentioned in verse 11 shall last—that is, "till we all come . . . unto the measure of the stature of the fulness of Christ." This statement does not mean that all the offices mentioned in verse 11 are permanent, for we have already observed that apostles and prophets ceased to be after the first Christian generation. It does mean, however, that the ministries rendered by those offices have abiding significance.

"Come" translates a Greek verb which is here used figuratively. It means "to arrive," in the sense of reaching a goal.

The goal itself is described by the prepositional phrases which begin: "in . . . unto . . . unto . . ." (v. 13). First then, the goal of growth is said to be the attainment by the whole body of Christ of "the unity of the faith, and of the knowledge of the Son of God" (v. 13, ASV). "Unity" is to be taken with both "faith" and "knowledge," and the latter two words are both modified by "of the Son of God." What Paul contemplates is a oneness of faith in, and a oneness of knowledge which concerns, the Son of God. The word "faith" is to be taken in the sense of trust and confidence. The Greek word for "knowledge" is a particularly strong one, denoting full, accurate, and true knowledge.

The goal is further expressed by the words, "unto a perfect

[full-grown, mature] man." What is meant by attaining unto a perfect man is explained by the added phrase, "unto the measure of the stature of the fulness of Christ." That is to say, for the whole company of the redeemed to reach mature manhood in a spiritual sense is for them to attain to the measure of the full stature of Christ, complete conformity to Christ being the ultimate standard of perfection. The idea is not mainly that of individual believers attaining to perfection but rather that of the church, made up of the whole body of believers and viewed as a single organism, reaching its full spiritual stature. "The Church is already the fulness of Christ by the call of God (Eph. 1:23); now she is to attain that fulness in the spiritual growth and life of her members." [3]

This goal, in the fullest sense, will not become a reality until the end of time, when the church as the bride of Christ stands before him "glorious," "not having spot, or wrinkle, or any such thing" (Eph. 5:27). Verses 14–16, however, appear to contemplate at least a relative fulfilment in time.

(2) *The result of attaining the goal* (*vv. 14–16*).—Verse 13 has given a general statement of the goal of growth set before God's people; verses 14–16 now set forth the result of attaining that goal. One may think of numerous benefits which issue from the attainment of spiritual maturity, but the one thing uppermost in Paul's mind was doctrinal stability. When we arrive at the measure of the full stature of Christ we are no longer infants at the mercy of error. Paul put it like this: ". . . no longer children, tossed to and fro [like waves of the sea], and carried about with [by] every wind of doctrine" (ASV). "Children" is in contrast with the "perfect man" of verse 13. "Tossed to and fro, and carried about" are words that might be used of a ship abandoned on a storm-tossed sea—a graphic figure of instability and helplessness. "Wind of doctrine" suggests the shifting currents of false teaching, blowing now from this quarter, now from that. To be "carried about by every wind of doctrine" is to be swept along by

whatever religious currents may be blowing most strongly at the time.

The particular "wind of doctrine" Paul had in mind for his time was the incipient gnosticism which was threatening the churches of Asia when he wrote this letter. Combining a bare minimum of Christian truth with Jewish ritualism and Oriental mysticism, this heresy perverted the doctrine of salvation by grace, misconstrued the character of the Christian life, and cast a shadow over the glory and majesty of Jesus Christ. Against this system of error Paul warned the Colossians: "Beware lest any man spoil you through philosophy and vain deceit, after the tradition of men, after the rudiments of the world, and not after Christ" (2:8).

Persons who lack spiritual stability, whether they live in the first or the twentieth century, are always easy prey for peddlers of religious fads and heresies. They have, as Eadie says, "just enough Christian intelligence to unsettle them, and make them the prey of every idle suggestion, the sport of every religious novelty." [4]

False teaching wields its peculiar power "by the sleight of men, and [by] cunning craftiness" (v. 14). The word translated "sleight" originally meant "dice-throwing." It came to be a term for clever trickery and deception, which is its meaning here. "Cunning craftiness" translates a word which betokens a readiness to do anything. It describes people who will stop at nothing in their effort to ensnare gullible and fickle souls. What a vivid description of the malicious ways of error!

What is stated negatively in verse 14 is stated positively in verse 15. The former verse has shown that to arrive at mature spiritual manhood means to be no longer infants at the mercy of error. Verse 15 puts the same thought in terms of adherence to truth and growing up to Christ.

The language of verse 16 is very compact and highly

figurative. It pictures the body of Christ (the church) as an "organism in which each member contributes to the growth of the whole by receiving and passing on the life drawn from Christ, the Head." [5] In this way the life and strength of the head flow into the body, permeating its every part. The main statement is: "The whole body . . . maketh increase [growth] of the body." Drawing from Christ, the body effects its own growth. And this process takes place "according to the effectual working in the measure of every part." The growth of the body of Christ is on the scale of, and in the manner of, the "working" or the proper functioning of each individual Christian (cf. v. 12).

ACTIVITIES FOR ENRICHMENT

List some factors which mar the unity of the Spirit in a church. Consider (silently, if you wish) which of these factors are present in your own church family. Engage in prayer for discernment about how to meet them.

[1] Charles Hodge, *A Commentary on the Epistle to the Ephesians* (Grand Rapids: Wm. B. Eerdmans Publishing Company, 1950), p. 212.

[2] *The New English Bible* (Oxford University Press; Cambridge University Press, 1961). Used by permission of the Clarendon Press, Oxford.

[3] F. F. Bruce, *The Epistle to the Ephesians* (New York: Fleming H. Revell Company, 1961), p. 87.

[4] John Eadie, *Commentary on the Epistle to the Ephesians* (reprint ed.; Grand Rapids: Zondervan Publishing House, n.d.), p. 316.

[5] Archibald M. Hunter, *The Layman's Bible Commentary* (Richmond: John Knox Press, 1959), XXII, 66–67. Used by permission.

CHAPTER 8

I. A CLEAN BREAK WITH OLD PAGAN WAYS (4:17–24)
  1. The Walk of the Gentiles (vv. 17–19)
  2. The Truth as It Is in Jesus (vv. 20–24)
    (1) Putting off the old man (v. 22)
    (2) Being renewed in the spirit of the mind (v. 23)
    (3) Putting on the new man (v. 24)

II. THE VIRTUES WHICH BECOME THE NEW MAN (4:25–32)

III. IMITATORS OF GOD (5:1–14)
  1. In Love (vv. 1–2)
  2. In Purity (vv. 3–6)
    (1) Sins to be avoided (vv. 3–4)
    (2) Reasons for avoiding sins of uncleanness (vv. 5–6)
  3. In Light (vv. 7–14)

IV. WALKING CIRCUMSPECTLY (5:15–21)
  1. By Redeeming the Time (v. 16)
  2. By Understanding the Will of God (v. 17)
  3. By Being Filled with the Spirit (vv. 18–21)

8

The Daily Walk of God's New People:
Moral Obligations

Ephesians 4:17 to 5:21

THE EPHESIAN LETTER pulsates with a double desire: that believers may have a fuller comprehension of what God in Christ is doing in and for them, and that their lives may in some measure correspond to his work of grace. In 4:1–16 Paul has dwelt upon those responsibilities which pertain especially to our relationships within the body of Christ. At verse 17 he turns to discuss duties, mostly of a moral nature, which concern our relation not only to fellow believers but more especially to the world about us. These are described first by a general statement (4:17–24) and then (4:25 to 5:21) in more detail.

I. A CLEAN BREAK WITH OLD PAGAN WAYS (4:17–24)

The use of the words "therefore" and "walk" (v. 17) points us back to the same words in 4:1. "Testify," a strong word of solemn appeal, means to insist or implore. The phrase "in the Lord" suggests that Paul is conscious of such a connection with the Lord that he speaks in the Lord's name and feels that his words are clothed with divine authority. The appeal itself is stated both negatively and positively. The negative part concerns the "walk" of the Gentiles (vv. 17–19); the positive part revolves around the concept of "truth [as it] is in Jesus" (vv. 20–24).

1. *The Walk of the Gentiles* (vv. 17–19)

Paul insists that his readers must "no longer walk as the Gentiles ... walk" (v. 17, ASV). He was saying to the recipients of this letter that they were no longer to be regarded as Gentiles. They were now "fellowcitizens with the saints" and a part of "the household of God." Their daily walk must conform to their new relationship. "No longer" implies that once they lived as the Gentiles. Now, however, they must renounce the life and wicked ways of their heathen neighbors.

The apostle proceeds to enumerate some of the salient features of pagan life in the first century—vanity, darkness, alienation, ignorance, hardness, loss of feeling, lasciviousness, uncleanness, greediness. It is a grim and revolting picture which he draws, in many respects parallel to the statement of Romans 1:18ff.

First, Paul speaks of "the vanity of their mind" (v. 17) and their being "darkened" in "the understanding" (v. 18). "Vanity" suggests emptiness, futility, and purposelessness—life with no real meaning, no goal. The thought is not that unregenerate minds are empty. It is that they are filled with things which lead to nothing. To have "the understanding darkened" is to be without the faculty of discernment, to be unable to distinguish right and wrong.

Next, non-Christians are described as "being alienated from the life of God" (v. 18). They are held in the grip of spiritual death, separated from the life which comes from God. The cause of this estrangement is twofold: "the ignorance that is in them" (v. 18) and "the blindness of their heart" (v. 18). Instead of the word "blindness" most modern versions have "hardness." The Greek word originally meant "petrifaction" but came eventually to be used by medical writers of numbness, insensibility, callousness. Here it betokens an insensitivity to spiritual things.

"Being past feeling" (v. 19) continues the idea suggested

by "hardness." The word primarily means "to cease to feel pain," then "to cease to care"—whether through despair or through recklessness. In this passage it describes reckless abandon, a state of moral insensibility wherein one no longer feels the reproaches of conscience.

Being thus destitute of compunctions, pagan people gave "themselves over unto lasciviousness, to work all [every kind of] uncleanness with greediness" (v. 19). Two frightful words are used in this statement. The first is "lasciviousness," the Greek of which denotes lewd or wanton conduct which shocks public decency. The man who can be so described no longer cares to hide his sin; it does not matter to him who sees his shame so long as he can gratify his desires. The word translated "greediness" is built on a root which means "to have more." The Greek word describes a disposition which has absolutely no regard for the rights of others. It is very wide in scope, being used sometimes in reference to material things (translated "covetousness") and sometimes of such things as sexual indulgence (translated "greediness"), as here. "It is the spirit of the man," explains Barclay, "who does not care whom he hurts and what method he uses so long as he gets what he desires."[1]

Commenting on this description of ancient pagan life, one writer asks whether Paul "put too much lampblack into his painting." He goes on to say:

Let us answer this question with another one: If Paul were writing today, would his picture of those who live the pagan life be much rosier? Some cultured humanists of our day who repudiate the Christian faith undoubtedly lead morally respectable lives; but not all. A goodly number of them dislike Christianity not so much for intellectual as for moral reasons, namely, because it insists on purity and chastity. In any case, no clear-sighted observer of our human situation can deny that when men and women reject the blessings and sanctions of Christianity, they relapse into ways of living not unlike Paul's Gentiles. Who will dare to say that "the world" today (which is the equivalent of "the Gentiles" in our letter) is not full of drunkenness, gambling, sexual vice, and that ruthless self-assertion which cares nothing for its neighbor's rights? [2]

2. The Truth as It Is in Jesus (vv. 20–24)

The "ye" (v. 20) is in sharp contrast to the "Gentiles" (v. 17). The force of the Greek may be brought out by translating: "But you—you did not thus learn the Christ." The readers of this letter did indeed learn the Christ, but not in such way as to condone their old pagan habits. When they received the gospel they were taught that Christian discipleship required the renunciation of all pagan vices and the cultivation of true Christian holiness.

The readers had been taught "truth [as it] is in Jesus" (v. 21, ASV). No article is used with "truth" in the Greek, the thought being that whatever is truth or spiritual reality is embodied in Christ. Such truth can be known only by those who have "learned Christ," have "heard him," and have been "taught by him" (vv. 20–21).

The essence of truth as it is in Jesus is defined in the Greek by three infinitive clauses. In the English text these infinitives are expressed by the words "put off" (v. 22), "be renewed" (v. 23), and "put on" (v. 24).

(1) Putting off the old man (v. 22).—A part of truth as it is in Jesus is that "ye [did] put off [once for all] concerning the former conversation [manner of life] the old man" (v. 22). The "old man" is an important phrase. Romans 6:6 affirms that "our old man is crucified with" Christ. Colossians 3:9 asserts, "Ye have put off the old man with his doings" (ASV). The term personifies the moral and spiritual state of the pre-Christian life (cf. Gal. 2:20). Moule understands it to mean "all that I was as an unregenerate son of Adam, liable to eternal doom, and the slave of sin." [3]

The "old man" is not renewed, is not converted. He is under sentence of death and is in process of decaying. He grows more and more "corrupt" by virtue of the deceitful lusts that belong to his nature (v. 22). The only remedy is to renounce him completely, nail him to the cross, and replace him with the "new man" (v. 24). When Paul speaks of putting off the old man, the figure is that of stripping off a garment. The tense points to a definite, decisive, and permanent act.

(2) *Being renewed in the spirit of the mind* (*v. 23*).— Truth as it is in Jesus teaches that believers are being continually "renewed in the spirit [disposition] of" the "mind" (v. 23). This renovation should be compared with "the vanity" of mind which marked the Gentiles (v. 17). The word for "be renewed" is a present tense, denoting something continuous and progressive in the life of the believer. It represents an experience which is the antithesis of the growing corruptness of the old man.

(3) *Putting on the new man* (*v. 24*).—Finally, truth as it is in Jesus means "that ye [did] put on [once for all] the new man" (v. 24). This statement is the positive counterpart of the negative in verse 22. The old man was stripped off; the new man is "put on." The two acts are absolutely inseparable.

This new self of the believer has been created "after [the likeness of] God" "in righteousness and holiness of truth" (v. 24, ASV). Righteousness in this context likely refers to our manward behavior, right dealing between man and man. Holiness, on the other hand, has to do with our conduct toward God. Both are the proper fruit of embracing the truth as it is in Jesus.

II. The Virtues Which Become the New Man (4:25–32)

The "wherefore" (v. 25) shows that the detailed instructions which follow are rooted in, and grow out of, the principles set forth in 4:20–24. Christians, in principle, put off the old man and put on the new at conversion. But what is true already in principle must be made real in actual practice. The new nature imparted at conversion must be cultivated; the old must be subdued.

In verses 25–32 five classes of sins, viewed as the rags which belonged to the old man, are mentioned; the corresponding virtues, viewed as the robes which should adorn the new man, are set in striking contrast.

First, "lying" must be banished from the Christian's life, and in its place "truth" must be cultivated (v. 25). "Lying"—the word includes every kind of deception—is one of the chief characteristics of the old man. It is pre-eminently a heathen vice, as missionaries from pagan lands abundantly testify. Unfortunately it is not confined to pagan lands. People in a so-called Christian culture need also to be admonished at this point. We see on every hand dishonesty in personal relations, unscrupulous practices in business, and corruption and deception in government.

Second, sinful anger must be controlled and subdued (vv. 26–27). There is a place for anger of a certain sort in the Christian life. (Cf. Mark 3:5.) But this permission concerning anger is strongly qualified by two additional statements. It must be carefully guarded so as not to pass into sin (v. 26). Anger that is selfish, undisciplined, and uncontrolled is always sinful. What starts out as righteous indignation all too easily degenerates to this level. Anger must never be cherished: "Let not the sun go down upon your wrath" (v. 26). Anger that is not speedily deposed soon takes deep root in the heart. When this happens the devil—"slanderer" is the meaning of the Greek word—gains "room to act," a foothold from which to exploit us (v. 27).

A third vice which has no place in the Christian life is stealing (v. 28). Paul had in mind the person who was a thief before his conversion and may have been in danger of falling back into his old ways. Instead of this, he is encouraged to engage in honest toil so that he not only meets his own needs but may have something to share with those less fortunate than himself.

"Corrupt communication" (v. 29), the fourth vice to be

named, may be understood as either foulmouthed talk or
worthless speech. Such language had likely been habitual
with many of Paul's readers before their conversion. It is
unbecoming for a Christian and must be completely re-
nounced. The suppression of bad language, however, is not
enough. Conscious effort is to be made to use language that
will edify and "minister grace [benefit] unto the hearers"
(v. 29).

Verse 30 is to be taken in the closest possible connection
with what has been said in the preceding verses. The point
is that lying, resentment, stealing, and especially the use of
filthy, unedifying language by Christians grieve the indwelling Spirit. This fact explains the misery of many believers,
for it is precisely by reason of permitting such practices that
they have lost the joy, peace, and blessedness that once they
knew. Cowper referred to such an experience when he wrote:

> Where is the blessedness I knew
>   When first I saw the Lord?
> Where is the soul refreshing view
>   Of Jesus and His Word?
>
> What peaceful hours I then enjoyed!
>   How sweet their mem'ry still!
> But they have left an aching void
>   The world can never fill.
>
> Return, O Holy Dove, return,
>   Sweet messenger of rest;
> I hate the sins that made Thee mourn,
>   And drove Thee from my breast.

The list of sins in verse 31 all have to do with bad temper.
"Bitterness" describes the sour, resentful spirit of a person
who broods over the injuries and slights he receives and re-
fuses to be reconciled. "Wrath" is literally a sudden outburst
of passion; "anger" is a settled feeling. Such eruptions of
temper show themselves both in "clamour" and in "evil speaking." The first of these words likely refers to public quar-

reling; the latter word may be taken in this context to mean slanderous whispers. These things, together "with all malice" are to be decisively "put away." The Greek word for "malice" may be defined as "a vicious disposition" or "spite." Moule understands it as "the deep *unkindness* of the self-centered, Christless heart."[4] Certainly, it should have no place in a believer's life.

The vacuum created when these vices are ejected from the heart is to be filled by the lovely virtues of kindness, tenderheartedness, forgiveness, and love (v. 32). "Kind" translates a Greek word, the root of which means useful or helpful. To be "tenderhearted" is to have a compassionate feeling toward the weaknesses and miseries of others. "Forgiving" is the rendering of a word of unusually rich content. Being built on the same root as the word for "grace," it first means "to give freely," then "to pardon" or "forgive." The supreme example as well as the sacred incentive for this attitude is that which God has done for us—as Paul puts it, "even as God for Christ's sake [literally, "in Christ," i.e., acting in Christ] hath forgiven you" (v. 32).

III. Imitators of God (5:1–14)

The appeal to "be . . . followers [imitators] of God, as dear children" is the main thought of 5:1–14. The idea is that we are to imitate God because we are his children. Such imitation, then, is not the means of our acceptance with God but the result of it.

1. *In Love* (vv. 1–2)

Paul's word is: "Walk in love, as Christ also hath loved us" (v. 2). There are two distinguishing marks of this love. The first, forgiveness, is implied from the closing verse of chapter 4. God in Christ has forgiven you (4:32); you then, as his beloved children, are to be imitators of him and cherish a forgiving spirit toward one another (5:1).

A second mark of this love is sacrifice, "Christ also hath loved us, and hath given himself for us" (v. 2). This love is not mere sentiment and feeling. It is love that gives all, that counts no sacrifice too great for the object on which it is fixed.

2. *In Purity* (vv. 3–6)

Regulated as it was by the will of God, Christ's was a holy love which could never tolerate evil and had in it no admixture of impurity. This thought leads Paul to warn especially against sins of uncleanness.

(1) *Sins to be avoided* (*vv. 3–4*).—The sins to be especially avoided are listed in two groups, each containing three related vices. Mention is made of "fornication, and all uncleanness, or covetousness." These iniquitous vices are to be so far removed from Paul's readers that they are not even to be "named among" them (v. 3). Paul means that these sins are to be so foreign to Christians that not the slightest intimation or suspicion of their presence among them can occur.

The Greek word for "fornication" originally denoted the practice of consorting with prostitutes, but it came to signify any form of sexual evil. The Gentile world of Paul's day regarded this sin as a matter of moral indifference, and it was indulged in without scruple by all classes of people. Infidelity in marriage was frightfully common, and homosexuality had for centuries been an accepted way of life. Some of the great pagan temples were staffed by hundreds of priestesses who were nothing more than religious prostitutes placed there for the use of the men who came to offer their licentious worship to heathen deities.

"All uncleanness" and "covetousness" go together, the "or" that joins them indicating that though they are different sins they belong to the same class. "Uncleanness" is nearly always used in the New Testament in a moral sense. "All uncleanness" is to be understood in the sense of every kind of sexual immorality. "Covetousness," which is considered very lightly

by many people today, is unsparingly condemned in the New
Testament and is several times classed by Paul with the gross-
est kinds of immorality. So diluted has our thinking become
that one sometimes hears it said of a person, "He is a good
Christian. His only fault is covetousness." In light of the
present passage it might be just as proper to describe a
woman as both a virtuous lady and an infamous prostitute.

Verse 4 lists three other kindred sins: "Neither filthiness,
nor foolish talking, nor jesting" are to be named among believers. The word translated by "filthiness" appears here to
refer to indecent, shameful speech—possibly to filthy stories.
"Foolish talking" includes not only coarse vulgarity but all
idle gossip as well. The Greek word means "fool-talk" and
suggests that those who jest of unclean things and in general
engage in debasing conversation demonstrate that they are
fools. "Jesting" should be understood as denoting buffoonery
and ribaldry. Paul is not condemning lively and sanctified
humor. He is not calling upon us to be long-faced, gloomy
people who dare not tell anything which evokes innocent
laughter. A good, hearty laugh is often medicine for the soul.
But there are some things of which Christians should never
make jokes—some are too sacred, some too filthy.

In the words "which are not convenient" (v. 4), Paul gathers up filthiness, foolish talking, and jesting, and describes
them as things not seemly for believers. True Christian cheer-
fulness and buoyancy of spirit should manifest itself "rather"
in "giving of thanks" (v. 4).

(2) *Reasons for avoiding sins of uncleanness* (vv. 5–6).—
Paul has used stern words about sins of uncleanness. Their
utter incongruity with Christian profession is now brought
out by two further considerations: the character of God's
kingdom and the fact of God's wrath.

The character of God's kingdom is such that "no whoremonger, nor unclean person, nor covetous man . . . hath any

inheritance" in it (v. 5). Those who are so described show a character wholly incompatible with that divine kingdom into which only the regenerate may enter (John 3:3). Their lives bear witness to the fact that they are strangers to grace and are still held in "the gall of bitterness, and in the bond of iniquity."

The "whoremonger" is one who practices any kind of sexual immorality. In this context the "unclean person" must be the person whose life is marked by sexual impurity. The "covetous man" is "an idolater" because in his greed for things—whether material or sensual—he sets up in his heart an object of worship other than God.

The "kingdom . . . of God" is the redemptive rule of God which delivers men from the powers of evil and brings to them "righteousness, and peace, and joy in the Holy Ghost" (Rom. 14:17). The church, which is not to be identified with the kingdom, is the fellowship of those who have accepted Christ's offer of the kingdom and have submitted to its rule. In a sense, the kingdom creates the church and the church is the instrument for extending the kingdom. It is here called "the kingdom of Christ" because God has committed the administration of it to Christ's hands (Luke 22:29). In a sense, the redemptive rule of God is embodied in him. In his person and mission that rule has already invaded human history (Matt. 3:2; 12:28) and is now moving toward a glorious consummation when Christ, having put all his enemies under his feet, will return the kingdom to the Father (1 Cor. 15:24–28).

A second reason for avoiding sins of uncleanness is the fact of God's wrath (v. 6). Apparently there were not wanting in Paul's day (and surely not in our day) those persons who, by specious arguments, would excuse and condone the sins under discussion. Paul may have had in mind those who were influenced by gnosticism to believe that sins of the body could not affect the soul and therefore had no bearing on the spiritual life. Or, he may allude to those who felt that freedom from law meant license to sin.

The readers are warned against letting anyone, whoever he may be, lead them astray by "vain [empty] words." Such words are void of all truth and reality and if heeded can only lead to spiritual tragedy. It is because of these very sins that "the wrath of God" comes "upon the children of disobedience" (cf. 2:2-3). The tense of the verb "cometh" is present and strongly suggests the certainty of the divine visitation upon the workers of iniquity.

3. *In Light* (vv. 7-14)

Paul's readers are urgently enjoined not to become partners in sin with those upon whom the wrath of God must inevitably fall. If they recoil from partnership in their punishment, let them also recoil in horror from partnership in their sins (v. 7).

A third area in which we are to imitate God is in light. Once the readers were "darkness," but now they were "light in the Lord" (v. 8). In their unconverted state, ignorance and sin had so penetrated their being that they were not merely in the dark; they were the very embodiment of darkness. Conversely, in their converted state the light of the gospel had so penetrated them that they were themselves light. In them the light had become visible and was the dominant trait of their character. The meaning of the verse is brought out in its contrasts—"sometimes" (better, "once") and "now"; "darkness" and "light." The emphasis, however, rests upon "were," which in the Greek is the first word of its clause. To say that the readers *were* darkness is to imply that deeds of darkness are now behind them. Such things are no longer in harmony with their character, and they must not revert to them.

Three responsibilities are rooted in this concept of believers being "light in the Lord." First, they are to "walk as children of light" (v. 8). Their conduct must conform to that which is most essential in their character.

Second, those who are light in the Lord are to produce the fruit of the light. This fruit is defined as "goodness and righteousness and truth" (v. 9, ASV). These may be called the cardinal qualities that mark life in the light. The Greek word translated by "goodness" stresses kindliness and benevolence, the spirit that makes one want to help others. "Righteousness" is regard for the rights of others, giving both to men and to God that which is their due. "Truth" concerns not only what is spoken; it is truth of idea, sincerity, straightforwardness.

The third responsibility of the children of light is to reprove "the unfruitful works of darkness" (vv. 11–14). Such works are "unfruitful" (v. 11) because they produce no goodness, give no satisfaction and joy (cf. v. 9). To "reprove" (v. 11) the works of darkness is to expose them, to turn the light upon them and show that they are unfruitful and belong to the darkness. It is not enough merely to withdraw, to "have no fellowship with" them. The light of believers must blaze out into the darkness and be a constant condemnation of the darkness.

Verse 12 tells why it is imperative to reprove the works of darkness: They are so unspeakably bad, especially those done secretly, that the Christian has no other recourse.

Verse 13, a very difficult verse which is variously translated, offers still another reason for reproving the deeds of darkness. The idea seems to be: Your responsibility is to reprove these things, for you are light, and light is that which makes manifest.

Verse 14, which is introduced as a quotation, is understood by many interpreters to express the substance of Isaiah 60:1. By others it is thought to be a quotation from an early Christian hymn. Either way, it may be taken as an example of the way in which reproof is to be administered. That is, the reproof of sinners is to take the form of an urgent call to them to let the light of Christ shine upon them. Its aim is never to be mere rebuke; it seeks the conversion of the sinner.

IV. WALKING CIRCUMSPECTLY (5:15-21)

This portion of the Ephesian letter constitutes an exhortation to the readers to live like wise men. "See then that ye walk circumspectly, not as fools, but as wise" (v. 15). "Circumspectly" suggests looking all around, giving attention to all circumstances and consequences as one might do when passing through a very dangerous place. It expresses the idea of living in strict conformity to a standard, guarding against anything which would be improper or unbecoming for the Christian. The thought is further explained by the words "not as fools, but as wise." It may be translated, "Watch carefully, then, how you walk." Believers are to walk as people having the character of wise men, not fools.

1. *By Redeeming the Time* (v. 16)

In verses 16-21 the walk of wisdom is defined in three particulars. First, it means that one will make the most of every opportunity—"redeeming the time" (v. 16). "Redeeming" is a market term meaning "to buy out" or "purchase completely." "Time" is the translation of a Greek word which came to mean something rather like "opportunity." To "buy out the opportunity" is to make the most of the time, to pay the price in effort and exertion that is necessary in using it.

The Greeks represented the concept of opportunity in sculpture by a youth with wings on his feet and back, having long hair in front and being bald in back. The suggestion was that if he is grasped at all he must be grasped by the forelock. So, opportunities for Christian service are brief seasons that soon slip by. The wise Christian will recognize them and use them while he can.

2. By Understanding the Will of God (v. 17)

The primary consideration for the Christian must never be what is most profitable financially, what is most pleasurable or enjoyable, or what will bring the greatest personal advantage or honor. His first concern is to discern what God wills him to be and to do. This course is the way of wisdom, and anything short of it betrays a mind lacking in moral intelligence.

3. By Being Filled with the Spirit (vv. 18–21)

Verse 18 contains both a negative and a positive command: "Be not drunk with wine, wherein is excess; but be filled with the Spirit." Drunkenness is alluded to as a concrete example of the heedless folly referred to in verse 17. It is forbidden because it leads to "excess" or dissoluteness. John Eadie's words, written long ago, are still all too true. Speaking of intemperance, he declared that there is in it

that kind of dissoluteness which brooks no restraint, which defies all efforts to reform it, and which sinks lower and lower into hopeless and helpless ruin. . . . This tremendous sin . . . is all the more to be shunned as its hold is so great on its victims, for with periodical remorse there is periodical inebriety; the fatal cup is again coveted and drained; while character, fortune, and life are risked and lost in the gratification of an appetite of all others the most brutal in form and brutifying in result. There are few vices out of which there is less hope of recovery—its haunts are so numerous and its hold is so tremendous.[5]

The emphasis of the verse, however, falls on the positive command, "Be filled with the Spirit." The Greek text, which reads literally, "Be filled in Spirit," suggests that the Spirit is the element *in* which we are to be filled. The thought is that of the Spirit so surrounding and possessing one's being that he is controlled and impelled by the Spirit. This experience should not be looked upon as exceptional, nor as the preroga-

tive of only a select few. It is considered by Paul the normal
state of every believer. Careful study of the Acts, where the
idea of the fulness of the Spirit is especially prominent, leads
to the conclusion that the being filled with the Spirit was repeated from time to time and that the supreme condition was
full surrender to Christ.

Carnal intoxication leads to dissoluteness, but the fulness
wrought by the Spirit of God issues in joyfulness (v. 19),
thankfulness (v. 20), and mutual submission (v. 21).

"Speaking to yourselves in psalms and hymns and spiritual
songs" is a general expression of glad and cheerful discourse,
defined more precisely by the phrase, "singing and making
melody in [with] your heart to the Lord" (v. 19). Those who
are filled with the Spirit express among themselves their joyous emotions in psalms, hymns, and spiritual songs. The reference may be both to social conversation and to meetings of
divine worship. Both are to be marked by hallowed and joyful
praise.

Too sharp a distinction between "psalms," "hymns," and
"songs" should not be drawn. The language is intended to
emphasize rich variety of sacred song, not to give instruction
in ancient hymnology. If any differentiation is made, "psalms"
may be taken to refer to Old Testament psalms, while
"hymns" and "spiritual songs" both refer to distinctively Christian compositions, the latter possibly being impromptu rhyth-
mic utterances produced under the influence of the Holy
Spirit.

"With your heart" (ASV) indicates that these joyful expressions are not to be merely mechanical productions of lip and
finger. Unless our praise springs from the heart it is not acceptable to the Lord.

The mention of joyful praise leads naturally to the mention of thanksgiving as another expression of the fulness of
the Spirit. Four things are said: It is to be constant, "always."
It is "for all things." It is "unto God." It is "in the name of

our Lord Jesus Christ" (v. 20). This note of thanksgiving re-
curs again and again in Ephesians, Colossians, and Philippians.

"Submitting yourselves one to another" (v. 21) denotes that
attitude of reciprocal deference which becomes and marks
out those who are filled with the Spirit. It is opposed to rude-
ness, haughtiness, selfish preference for one's own opinions,
and stubborn insistence on one's own rights. Paul expressed
much the same thought in Romans 12:10, "in honour pre-
ferring one another."

In verse 21 the general rule of mutual submission is stated;
in 5:22 to 6:9 the principle is applied to specific relations.
The verse thus concludes the present section and forms the
connecting link with the next paragraph.

ACTIVITIES FOR ENRICHMENT

Reverently, would you like to pantomime the figures used to express the truth in Ephesians 4:17–32?

How could one portray in a picture the ideas in the words:
walking circumspectly; redeeming the time?

---

[1] William Barclay, *The Letters to the Galatians and Ephesians* (Philadelphia: The Westminster Press, 1958), p. 182.

[2] Archibald M. Hunter, *The Layman's Bible Commentary* (Richmond: John Knox Press, 1959), XXII, 67. Used by permission.

[3] H. C. G. Moule, "The Epistle to the Ephesians," *The Cambridge
Bible for Schools and Colleges* (Cambridge: The University Press,
1887), p. 118.

[4] _____, *Ephesian Studies* (New York: Fleming H.
Revell Company, n.d.), p. 235.

[5] John Eadie, *Commentary on the Epistle to the Ephesians* (reprint
ed.; Grand Rapids: Zondervan Publishing House, n.d.), p. 397.

CHAPTER 9

alcohol —

9

The Daily Walk of God's New People:
Domestic Obligations

Ephesians 5:22 to 6:9

IF YOU WERE ASKED to name three or four things which today constitute the gravest threats to family life, what would your list include? Worldly concepts of marriage? Godlessness in the home? Changing views concerning sexual morality? Parental irresponsibility? The usurpation by other institutions of the prerogatives of the home? The hurried, frantic pattern of modern-day life? Television?

In a sobering chapter entitled "The Withering Away of the Family," Elton and Pauline Trueblood write: "Of all the disintegrating factors the chief is the loss of the sense of meaning of what a family ought to be. Our basic failure is not the failure to live up to a standard that is accepted, but rather the failure to keep the standard clear!" [1]

In this classic passage (5:22 to 6:9) Paul clearly delineates the standard. Beginning with the principle of mutual submission based on reverence for Christ (v. 21), the apostle proceeds to mention the reciprocal duties of the various members of the household—wives and husbands, children and parents, slaves and masters.

I. THE WIFE'S DUTY TO THE HUSBAND (5:22–24)

The one wifely duty which Paul insists upon is that of submission: "Wives, submit yourselves unto your own husbands" (v. 22). His words are a text on the Christian marriage relation. Clearly, Paul does not mean that the husband is to be a domestic despot, ruling his family with a rod of iron. But the husband exercises an authority which the wife must forego. In areas where one must yield—for example, the husband's choice of a profession or of a geographical location for his work—the primary submission must devolve upon the wife.

Many people today object that such a view of marriage is not appropriate for twentieth-century society. Careful consideration of the present passage, however, should remove all uneasiness about this duty of the wife to her husband.

The context clearly shows that the wife's submission is prompted by and warranted by the husband's unselfish love. No wife need have any misgivings about subordinating herself to a husband who loves her with the same kind of sacrificing love that Christ has for the church.

The submission is to be voluntary. The form used in the Greek makes the statement of verse 22 something less than a positive command; it is rather an earnest appeal. The Greek word uses the middle voice, which is best translated "submitting *yourselves*." The wife's submission is not something forced upon her by a demanding husband; it is the deference that a loving wife, conscious that home (just as any other institution) must have a head, gladly shows to a worthy and devoted husband.

This submission of the wife is presented as a part of her Christian duty, a self-subjection to be rendered "as unto the Lord" (v. 22). The meaning is not that she is to yield to her husband the same submission which she gives to Christ. The thought is that the deference given to her husband is a duty which she owes to the Lord. Just as believers form one body of which Christ is head, so the married couple constitute a unity of which the husband is to be head. To ignore this divine arrangement is to sow seeds of domestic discord and tragedy.

Paul is careful to point out, however, that in one supreme respect the headship of Christ over the church differs from that of the husband over the wife. "He [the pronoun is emphatic] is the saviour of the body [i.e., the church]" (v. 23). Christ as Saviour of his church is to the church what no husband can ever be to his wife.

The subordination of the wife to her husband is to be patterned after that of the church for Christ (v. 24). Believers do not require the compulsion of a divine command but joyfully and willingly subject themselves to Christ. So should it be with the wife in her relation to her husband. The phrase "in every thing" is clearly limited by the context to those things pertaining to home relations. Even in this respect the rule must be qualified by the principle of allegiance to Christ. Higher obligations always take precedence over the lower.

II. THE HUSBAND'S DUTY TO THE WIFE (5:25–33)

The ancient world was a man's world, and in no place was this point of view more apparent than in the home. Among the Jews the wife was often little more than chattel. The Greeks confined the women of the household to their own quarters and did not even permit them to eat their meals with the men. Paul's instructions are in striking contrast to all of this, for he recognizes that even the husband has duties within the home.

The supreme duty enjoined upon the husband is that he love his wife. The word employed does not denote mere affection or romantic attachment; it speaks of a higher form of love, a deliberate attitude of mind which concerns itself with the well-being of the one loved. Self-devotion, not self-satisfaction, is its dominant trait. It is, in short, a love which makes it a delight for the wife to subject herself to such a husband.

How the husband is to love his wife, is set forth in three significant statements.

1. *As Christ Loved the Church* (vv. 25–27)

The measure of Christ's love is stated in the declaration that he "gave himself for" the church (v. 25). The husband is to love his wife in the same unstinted fashion, even to the point of sacrificing himself for her well-being.

The mention of Christ and the church led Paul to digress somewhat from his discussion of marriage. He points out that there was a twofold purpose in the self-sacrifice of Jesus. The first, an immediate purpose accomplished in the present age, is "that he might sanctify and cleanse it [the church] with the washing of water by the word." "Sanctify" means to set apart, to consecrate. "Cleanse" suggests the removal of sin and its defilement. The two acts are thought of as simultaneous, the cleansing being the means by which the sanctifying is effected.

Strenuous debate has revolved around the words "with the washing of water by the word" (v. 26). The "washing of water" is most naturally taken as a general reference to the symbolism of baptism. As an outward, physical act it pictures the inward, spiritual cleansing effected by Christ (cf. Titus 3:5). One may understand an allusion to the symbolism of baptism without in any way subscribing to the view that baptism actually effects a spiritual cleansing. The real cleansing comes through the application of the blood of Christ by the Holy Spirit in the new birth.

The expression "by the word" is even more difficult. Some take it to refer to the word of the gospel as the actual instrument by which the cleansing is accomplished (cf. John 15:3). Others interpret it as a spoken word accompanying the washing of water—"either the word which is spoken *over* the person being baptized . . . (cf. Matt. 28. 19 . . .), or (more probably) the word spoken *by* him, in which he confesses his faith and invokes the Lord" [2] (cf. Acts 22:16).

The second and ultimate purpose of Christ's death, to be realized fully at the end of the age, is set forth in verse 27: "that he might present it to himself a glorious church." The allusion is to a wedding ceremony, in which the bride is presented to her husband. The pronoun "he" stresses Christ's personal action. He himself, before the assembled universe, presents the bride to himself. (See Rev. 19:6–9 for John's description of the scene.)

The adjective "glorious," conveying here the thought of brilliant purity or moral splendor, shows the character in which the church is to be at last manifested—"not having spot, or wrinkle, or any such thing; but that it should be holy and without blemish." When the church is presented to her Lord there shall be nothing to mar her beauty—no spot of disfigurement, no wrinkle of age or decay, nor any other thing that might deform or defile. She is to be "holy" and "without blemish."

2. *As His Own Body* (vv. 28–30)

Verse 28 reiterates what verses 25–27 have already said, namely that Christ's love for his church is both model and incentive for the husband in his love for his wife. "As their own bodies" (v. 28) gives an added reason for husbandly love. Even as Christ loves the church, his body, in like manner ought husbands to love their wives, as being their own bodies. Husband and wife are complementary parts of one personality. Hodge explains the statement thus:

It does not indicate the measure of the husband's love, as though the meaning were, he should love his wife as much as he loves his own body. But it indicates the nature of the relation which is the ground of his love. He should love his wife, because she is his body.[3]

3. *With a Love Transcending All Other Human Relationships* (vv. 31–33)

The love which a man has for his wife must transcend even that which he has for parents, leading him to leave the latter and "be joined [glued] unto his wife" (v. 31). So intimate is this union that the man and woman thus joined together become "one flesh" (v. 31). In a day when divorce is scandalously easy, this concept of marriage needs often to be held before the public.

The mention of the closeness of the union of husband and wife again brought to Paul's mind the thought of the intimate spiritual union of Christ and his people (v. 32). The word "mystery," as elsewhere in the Ephesian letter, denotes a truth once hidden but now revealed. The mystery is "great" because it is both profoundly important and exceedingly wonderful.

In the light of the gospel Paul sees enshrined in the statement of Genesis 2:24 a great spiritual "mystery" concerning the union of Christ and his church. Verse 32 may be translated: "I for my part [the pronoun is emphatic to distinguish Paul from the writer of Gen. 2:24] am speaking with reference to Christ and with reference to the church." Thus, it is not marriage but the union between Christ and his church that Paul calls a mystery. It is the likeness of the conjugal union to this higher spiritual relationship that gives to marriage its deepest significance. Paul throughout the passage seems to be calling on husbands to measure up to the ideal of Christ in his love for the church, and to wives to measure up to the church in its devotion to Christ.

The Greek particle translated by "nevertheless" (v. 33) concludes the discussion about marriage and calls special attention to the main point. We may translate in this manner: "In any case each one of you must love his own wife as himself, and the wife must reverence [respect] her husband." The duty of the wife is to respect; the duty of the husband is to deserve that respect.

III. THE DUTY OF CHILDREN TO PARENTS (6:1–3)

Paul addresses himself to children, whose place in the home is another sphere in which the principle of submission operates. Two words sum up the child's duty to parents: "obey" and "honor." They are timely words for a day which tends to regard the freedom of the child as an absolute.

1. *Obedience* (v. 1)

The word translated by "obey" implies a readiness to hear and has the sense of obeying orders. The child is to listen to, and carry out, the commands of his parents.

This obedience is a Christian duty. This thought is conveyed by the words "in the Lord" (v. 1). They define the quality of obedience by setting forth the element or sphere in which it is to be performed. A certain sacredness is thus given to the obedience rendered by the children in a Christian home. It is prompted and regulated by a consciousness of Christian responsibility and must therefore be cheerful, prompt, and habitual.

Obedience is a moral duty. Children are to obey because "this is right" (v. 1). Filial obedience, therefore, is not based on anything accidental, nor does it depend essentially on the character of the parent. It is an obligation grounded in the very nature of the relationship between parents and children. It is a thing in itself right.

2. *Honor* (vv. 2–3)

The command to honor father and mother, quoted from the Decalogue, comprehends all the love, respect, and obedience which are involved in the filial relation. "Obedience," says Salmond, "is the *duty; honour* is the *disposition* of which the obedience is born."[4] (Note that this deep respect is to be paid to both "father and mother," an indication that the wife's place in the home is not a servile one.)

This commandment to honor parents is described as "the first commandment with promise" (v. 2). Probably Paul was thinking of the whole body of Mosaic legislation of which the Ten Commandments are the introduction. Possibly the word "first" has the sense of chief or primary: "a first commandment [i.e., one of primary importance] accompanied with a promise."

The promise itself is quoted in verse 3: "that it may be well with thee, and thou mayest live long on the earth." In their original setting (Ex. 20:12) these words apply to the nation Israel and have specific reference to prosperity and long life in the Promised Land. Paul gives the words a wider meaning, making them apply to all children who render obedience and honor to their parents.

Eadie understands Paul's use of these words to "involve a great principle, and that is, that filial obedience, under God's blessing, prolongs life, for it implies the possession of principles of restraint, sobriety, and industry, which secure a lengthened existence." [5]

Hodge points out that this promise, like all other such promises, "is a revelation of a general purpose of God, and makes known what will be the usual course of his providence. . . . Obedient children, as a general rule, are prosperous and happy. The general promise is fulfilled to individuals, just so far 'as it shall serve for God's glory, and their own good.'" [6]

IV. THE DUTY OF PARENTS TO CHILDREN (6:4)

Parental responsibility is stated in terms of the father's obligation. The suggestion is that the father as head of the household has a special responsibility in regard to the training of the children. No slight toward the mother is intended. Paul would be quick to recognize her rights and to acknowledge the molding power of her influence in the home.

"Children," wrote the psalmist, "are an heritage of the Lord" (Psalm 127:3). Their training and care should therefore be undertaken with a profound sense of responsibility to God. Two things are especially enjoined upon fathers. Negatively, they are cautioned not to "provoke" their children "to wrath" (v. 4). Parents are not to exercise their authority with unkindness and harshness.

It is said that Martin Luther's father was so stern that Luther found it difficult to pray, "Our Father." To him the word had a connotation of forbidding severity. "Spare the rod and spoil the child" he took to be wise counsel, but to keep others from having his own unpleasant childhood experience, he suggested keeping an apple beside the rod to give the child when he does well.

The authority of parents is for the child's good, not for their own selfish gratification. To make unreasonable demands of a child, to surround him with needless restrictions, or to punish him too severely will deaden his affections toward the parents and check his desires after holiness. Many a child has reached the point where he feels he cannot possibly please his parents and therefore decides that he need not try. It is a wise parent who seeks to make obedience easy for his children.

On the positive side, fathers are charged to bring up their children "in the nurture and admonition of the Lord" (v. 4). The word translated by "bring up" conveys here the idea of development in character. The word for "nurture" was used by the ancient Greeks of the general education of a child, of the whole course of training by which a boy was reared into a man. Moule understands it in the present text to include all "the wholesome *restraints* of a wise early education," "all training in the direction of a life modest, unselfish, and controlled."[7]

"Admonition" is a term containing the ideas of correction and warning, both of which parents owe to their children. The words "of the Lord" show that the training and correction of the child are to be exercised in a thoroughly Christian manner. It is training and correction administered by the parents, but proceeding from the Lord. The suggestion is that the Lord nurtures the child through the parents.

V. THE DUTY OF SLAVES TO MASTERS (6:5-8)

Paul had in mind the various relationships within the Christian household. The "servants" mentioned in this passage were bondslaves, not servants in the modern sense of the word. Slavery, with all its attendant evils, was universally accepted in ancient times. In fact, it was considered a fundamental institution, indispensable to civilized society. More than half the people seen on the streets of some of the great cities of the Roman world were slaves. They were people without rights, mere property existing only for the comfort, convenience, and pleasure of their owners. (Many of them were better educated and more cultured than their masters and were charged with the instruction of the children of the household.) Doubtless the early Christian churches numbered many slaves among their members.

It is a surprise to some people that the apostles did not denounce slavery in unequivocal language and demand its immediate and violent overthrow. But the apostles did not conceive of themselves primarily as social reformers; they were first and foremost heralds of the good news of salvation in Christ. Yet they did not condone slavery. Indeed, they announced the very principles (such as that of the complete spiritual equality of slave and master) which ultimately destroyed this terrible blot on civilization. The apostles' approach to this social evil was like that of a woodsman who strips the bark off a tree and leaves it to die. John Eadie puts it:

Christianity did not rudely assault the forms of social life, or seek to force even a justifiable revolution by external appliances.

Such an enterprise would have quenched the infant religion in blood. The gospel achieved a nobler feat. It did not stand by in disdain, and refuse to speak to the slave till he gained his freedom, and the shackles fell from his arms. . . . No; but it went down into his degradation, took him by the hand, uttered words of kindness in his ear, and gave him a liberty which fetters could not abridge and tyranny could not suppress.[8]

Paul points out that the slave-master relationship belongs only to the sphere of earthly things. The phrase, "masters according to the flesh" (v. 5) implies another relationship belonging to a higher, spiritual sphere where Christ is Master.

1. *The Manner in Which Obedience Is to Be Performed* (vv. 5–7)

The one duty urged upon slaves was that of obedience. They were to obey "with fear and trembling" (v. 5). This attitude was not to be abject terror, but the solicitous spirit of one having a true sense of responsibility and therefore eager to leave no duty undone.

Obedience was to be given "in singleness of . . . heart" (v. 5). It was to be done with inward reality and sincerity, without duplicity and pretense.

Obedience was to be "as unto Christ" (v. 5). The slave was to look upon his obedience as a kind of Christian duty, a service performed as unto the Lord himself. This point of view would lift it to the highest level and constitute strong motivation for carrying it out.

Verses 6–7 explain still further what it would mean for slaves to serve in the manner just described. They would not perform their duties "with eyeservice, as menpleasers" (v. 6). "Eyeservice" graphically depicts the conduct of the person who works only when he is watched. Such persons are "menpleasers," that is, workmen whose highest aim is to curry favor with their masters. Those who serve aright perform their duties "as the servants of Christ, doing the will of God from the heart; with good will doing service, as to the

Lord, and not to men." The believing slave was to see himself as Christ's slave and to understand that in the performance of his daily tasks he was doing God's will. For this reason his work was to be done heartily (literally, "out of the soul") and with "good will."

If Paul could write in this manner of the work of a person enslaved against his will, he would in even stronger language address himself to the modern-day employee who voluntarily enters into contract with an employer and receives remuneration for his work. Surely all that is said here of the fidelity and sincerity of slave service must with even greater force apply to free service.

2. *An Incentive for Obedience* (v. 8)

The participle "knowing" (v. 8) gives encouragement to the faithful performance of slave service. Earthly masters might take no note of faithful service rendered to them. But the Christian slave can know that his Heavenly Master will not fail to recompense his work. Every "good thing" done, whether by "bond or free," is known to the Lord and shall of his grace be rewarded.

VI. The Duty of Masters to Slaves (6:9)

Duty was not all on the side of slaves; Paul reminded masters that they also had obligations. In so doing he was giving expression to a very radical idea, for in that day it was commonly thought that slaves had no rights. Verse 9 contains three things: a principle, a prohibition, and an incentive for heeding these words of the apostle.

The principle is stated generally: "Ye masters, do the same things unto them." That is to say, act toward your slaves with the same regard to the will of God and the authority of Christ as has been enjoined on them.

The prohibition is to forbear "threatening." This admonition was most appropriate, for the common idea was that slaves must be kept in check by the fear of punishment. Christian masters must leave off this evil practice entirely. Those under their authority are to be treated always with respect and kindness, never with harshness. Does this admonition not say something regarding the treatment twentieth-century employers should give to those who work for them? Surely nothing less than the considerateness enjoined upon slaveholders becomes a present-day employer.

The incentive for acting in this manner (v. 9) might be rendered: "since you know that both their Master and yours is in heaven . . ." Christian masters are accountable to God for their treatment of slaves. Both they and their slaves bow alike before one Master, with whom there is no "respect of persons." "The gold ring of the master does not attract His eye, and it is not averted from the iron fetter of the slave." [9]

ACTIVITIES FOR ENRICHMENT

Thoughtfully sing or read all the words of Spitta's song, "O Happy Home Where Thou Art Loved." Follow with a season of prayer for the homes which your church is reaching and those which it should reach.

[1] Elton and Pauline Trueblood, *The Recovery of Family Life* (New York: Harper & Row, Publishers, Incorporated, 1953), pp. 18–19. Used by permission.

[2] F. F. Bruce, *The Epistle to the Ephesians* (New York: Fleming H. Revell Company, 1961), p. 116. Used by permission.

[3] Charles Hodge, *A Commentary on the Epistle to the Ephesians* (Grand Rapids: Wm. B. Eerdmans Publishing Company, 1950), p. 332.

[4] S. D. F. Salmond, *The Expositor's Greek Testament* (Grand Rapids: Wm. B. Eerdmans Publishing Company, n.d.), III, 375.

[5] John Eadie, *Commentary on the Epistle to the Ephesians* (reprint ed.; Grand Rapids: Zondervan Publishing House, n.d.), p. 442.

[6] Hodge, *op. cit.*, p. 359.

[7] H. C. G. Moule, "The Epistle to the Ephesians," *The Cambridge Bible for Schools and Colleges* (Cambridge: The University Press, 1887), p. 146.

[8] Eadie, *op. cit.*, p. 446.

[9] *Ibid.*, p. 455.

CHAPTER 10

I. THE CHRISTIAN WARFARE (6: 10–20)

1. The Believer's Strength (v. 10)
2. The Believer's Foe (v. 12)
3. The Believer's Protection (vv. 11,13–20)
   (1) The whole armor of God (vv. 11,13–17)
   (2) The practice of prayer (vv. 18–20)

II. THE CONCLUSION OF THE LETTER (6: 21–24)

1. An Explanation (vv. 21–22)
2. A Benediction (vv. 23–24)

10

The Holy Warfare of God's New People

Ephesians 6:10–24

IT IS A GRAVE MISTAKE to think that in the happy hour of our conversion all trouble and strife cease. In reality that hour marks the beginning of a lifelong warfare—not a war for our salvation, to be sure, but a war in Christian service. The closing portion of Paul's letter contains his account of this conflict of the Christian with the forces of evil.

I. THE CHRISTIAN WARFARE (6:10–20)

A note of tranquility pervades most of Ephesians. Beginning with a doxology of praise to God for the blessings of redemption, it proceeds to speak of the electing grace of God, the wonder of spiritual resurrection in Christ, the blissful indwelling of Christ in his people, and the pure and holy lives they are to live. The epistle closes, however, amid the din of battle with a rousing call to arms. For all the joys and for all the peace and happiness of the Christian life, it is nonetheless a life lived out on a spiritual battlefield.

Some commentators liken the Christian experience to life within a camp located in enemy territory. Within the camp the scene is one of loyalty, love, and fellowship. The ramparts, however, cannot for a moment be left unwatched. The saint must never live and move unarmed.

In the preceding section Christians have been singled out by groups, with special counsel for each. But what is said here is for all. Like a general leading an army against the enemy, Paul issues commands and gives instructions. He men-

129

tions the believer's strength (v. 10), his foe (v. 12), and his protection (vv. 11,13–17).

1. The Believer's Strength (v. 10)

As Paul thinks of the inevitable conflict, he charges Christians to be constantly filled with power. The word used, a particularly strong one suggesting the pouring of power into one, occurs also in Philippians 4:13: "I can do all things through Christ which strengtheneth [pours power into] me." The source of the strength needed is brought out by "in the Lord," the idea being that by virtue of our union with him the power that is inherently his may be drawn upon by us. In him we can do all things; apart from him defeat is inevitable.

What it means to be strong in the Lord is further explained by the phrase, "and in the power of his might." To be strong in the Lord is to be joined to the strength which belongs to his might. Observe the two leading words—"power" and "might." The former, which is used in the New Testament only of supernatural power—whether Satanic (Heb. 2:14) or divine (everywhere else)—denotes power as an active force, power exercised. The latter word, more passive in meaning, speaks of strength inherently possessed, whether exercised or not. This impressive accumulation of terms for strength, power, and might recalls 1:19, where Paul describes the exceeding greatness of the power of God available to believing people. Here, the readers are urgently exhorted to lay hold on that power in order to meet and vanquish the evil forces that assail them.

2. The Believer's Foe (v. 12)

In military strategy the failure to estimate properly the strength and capabilities of an enemy is a tragic mistake. In the Christian confrontation it is not only tragic but inexcusable, for we are clearly warned both of the nature of the conflict and of the formidable character of the enemy. "We wrestle not against flesh and blood." We are engaged in a life-and-death struggle, not against a frail human enemy but against the supernatural forces of evil. The word translated by "we wrestle" suggests hand-to-hand combat and thus magnifies the personal nature of the encounter.

"Principalities," "powers," "rulers," and "spiritual wickedness" are terms used here of the hierarchy of invisible powers in rebellion against God (cf. 1:21; 3:10). Paul is not to be understood as enumerating four different classes of demonic beings. Each term simply views the forces arrayed against God and his people in a different manner. "Principalities" refers to their rank and rule. "Powers" suggests their investment with authority. "World-rulers of this darkness" (ASV), points up their control over a world in revolt against its Creator (cf. 2 Cor. 4:4). "Spiritual wickedness in high places," or "spiritual hosts of wickedness in the heavenlies," depicts them as an army of wicked spirits inhabiting, or at least bringing their combat to, the heavenly sphere.

The phrase, "in the heavenlies" (cf. 1:3,20; 2:6; 3:10) may be interpreted as the *scene* of the conflict. So understood, the reference is to the heavenly sphere in which life in Christ is lived. The phrase may mean that the *abode* of the spiritual forces of wickedness is nonearthly, belonging to the invisible regions of the spirit world.

3. *The Believer's Protection* (vv. 11,13–20)

In another place Paul asserts that "the weapons of our warfare are not of the flesh, but mighty before God to the casting down of strongholds" (2 Cor. 10:4, ASV). The Christian finds protection in this mortal conflict by the use of the whole armor of God (vv. 11,13–17) and the practice of incessant prayer (vv. 18–20).

(1) *The whole armor of God* (*vv.* 11,13–17).—The expression "whole armour of God," employs the imagery of the Ro-

man man of arms fully equipped for heavy battle. It is the armor "of God" in the sense that it is armor which God provides. Each piece is furnished by him. It is called "the whole armour" to stress the completeness of it. We must see to it that no portion of our person is left exposed and unprotected.

God provides the armor, and it is ready for our use. But it is we who must, on our part, faithfully accept every instrument and implement which God offers. We are therefore urged to "put on" the whole armor of God in order that we "may be able to stand against the wiles of the devil" (v. 11). The tense of the verb "put on" denotes urgent and decisive action. When the enemy has already been engaged, it will be too late to arm ourselves. "To stand" in this context means not only to stand ready to fight but to hold one's ground. The "wiles of the devil" are his stratagems, the many and subtle ways by which he assails God's people. (See the use of "wiles" in 4:14, ASV.)

In verse 13 "wherefore," points back to the descriptions of verse 12 and calls attention to the menacing character of the enemy. He is so formidable in power that nothing less than the full armor of God will give ample protection. Instead of "put on" Paul here writes "take up" (ASV), the more common military expression for arming one's self. The suggestion is that the divine armor lies at the believer's feet ready for use; it needs only to be appropriated by him. The tense is again such as to denote urgency. Arms must be taken up at once in order for the Christian to be ready for any emergency.

The particular end in view is that the Christian "may be able to withstand in the evil day, and having done all, to stand" (v. 13). The word rendered by "to withstand" means to resist successfully. The "evil day" refers to those critical days of special trial or resolute satanic assault known to every child of God. As Maclaren observes, they are the days "when all the cannon belch at once, and scaling ladders are reared on every side of the fortress." The great preacher goes on to say that these days "are ever wont to come on us suddenly; they are heralded by no storm signals and no falling barometer. We may be like soldiers sitting securely round their camp fire, till all at once bullets begin to fall among them." [1] Against such days we must always be ready.

"Having done all" is a particularly strong expression meaning "having thoroughly done everything." The reference is not to the preparation for conflict but to the end of the conflict, when the enemy has been thoroughly vanquished. "To stand," speaks of the stance of victory. The thought is that the well-armed believer will be able to hold his ground. After the conflict is over, he does not lie prostrate in defeat but stands in complete possession of the field.

Salmond explains the idea in this fashion: "The spiritual warrior who has kept his position victorious and stood above his conquered foe in one 'evil day,' is to take his stand again ready to face another such critical day, should it come." [2] What is necessary to such a stand is expressed by four participles (ASV), each of which modifies the imperative "stand." These participles—"having girded" (v. 14), "having put on" (v. 14), "having shod" (v. 15), and "taking up" (v. 16)—speak of things which are to be done before one takes his stand.

The first piece of defensive armor is the girdle of truth (v. 14). The soldier's girdle was the belt or band which served to hold his tunic in place and from which the scabbard for his sword was suspended. "Truth" is without the article in the Greek text and therefore carries the idea of sincerity and truthfulness. It should be remembered, however, that this disposition of sincerity and truthfulness is not a natural quality; it is a supernatural grace, for the whole armor is of God.

Another essential part of the Roman soldier's equipment was the "breastplate," which, as its name suggests, protected the vital organs in the chest area. Without a breastplate a warrior was vulnerable to every assault of the enemy. Paul says that "righteousness" is the Christian's breastplate (v. 14).

This righteousness is sometimes understood to be the righteousness of justification, that which Paul elsewhere calls "the
righteousness of God" (Rom. 3:21) or "the righteousness
which is of God by faith" (Phil. 3:9). The word may here be
used, however, in a broad, general sense of moral rectitude,
meaning the believer's personal righteousness. This personal
righteousness which guards the heart is not possible apart
from the reception of God's justifying righteousness.

The well-equipped soldier in Paul's day wore sandals with
soles thickly studded with hobnails. Such sandals not only
gave protection to the feet but also enabled the soldier to
move quickly and surely. In ancient times, when warfare was
largely a matter of hand-to-hand combat, this quickness of
movement was essential. The Christian, Paul explains, must
have on his feet "the preparation of the gospel of peace" (v.
15). Most interpreters understand "preparation" in the sense
of "readiness" or "preparedness." The idea is that of a disposition of mind that makes men quick to see their duty and ever
ready to plunge into the fight. This readiness comes from, or
is produced by, "the gospel of peace."

The gospel is so designated because it is a peace-bringing
power which destroys the enmity in men's hearts and estab-
lishes tranquility in its place (cf. Isa. 52:7). It is this heart-
peace produced by the gospel that gives the Christian warrior
his readiness for combat. To have a consciousness of peace
with God and to live in tranquil communion with him enables
a man to fling himself into the battle with strong determination and calm assurance.

Next Paul names "the shield of [which is] faith," which
"above all" is to be taken up. "Above all" means simply "in
addition to all." (A variant reading of the Greek text, preferred by many scholars, employs a preposition which requires the phrase to be translated "in all things." If this
reading be followed, the meaning then must be that the shield
is to be taken up at every turn of the conflict.)

The "shield of faith" is an allusion not to the small round shield which was carried by cavalrymen but to the large oblong shield which the heavy-armed soldier carried. Behind it a man was fully protected. And that is the kind of shield, says Paul, that our conflict requires.

The "fiery darts"—among the most dangerous weapons used in ancient warfare—were arrows dipped in pitch or some other combustible material and set on fire before being thrown at the enemy. They could not only wound but also burn. The soldier's best protection—indeed, his only real protection—was to manipulate his shield so that these flaming missiles sank into its wood. Thus the missile was stopped and its fire was extinguished. "Faith," by which we must understand utter dependence upon God, affords like protection for the believer when he confronts Satan's most vicious attacks.

Faith protects us, however, not so much because of any inherent power which it has but because it brings us into touch with God and interposes him between the enemy and ourselves. By faith, therefore, we are enabled "to quench all the fiery darts of the wicked [one]," that is, the devil. Pay special attention to the word "all." In it there is ground for great confidence—not in ourselves, to be sure, but in God and in the strength which reliance upon him gives.

The last piece of defensive equipment to be named is "the helmet of [which is] salvation" (v. 17). Since Paul is addressing Christians the reference must be to the *consciousness* of salvation and the protection which such consciousness gives. The Christian warrior is commanded to "take" the helmet of salvation. This word, which is not the same as that used in reference to the shield, ordinarily means "to receive," "accept," or "welcome." In the present passage, however, it probably means "grasp."

The "sword of [supplied by] the Spirit" (v. 17) is the only offensive weapon in the panoply. But no other is needed. By it Christian (in Bunyan's allegory) put Apollyon to flight, and we shall find it more than adequate to meet our needs. In the last clause of verse 17 it is identified with "the word of God." This expression, the Greek of which more literally means "God's utterance," is not necessarily to be confined to the Bible. When Paul wrote this passage much of the New Testament had not yet come into being, and the Spirit was still speaking directly to the redeemed community apart from the written revelation (cf. Acts 11 : 28; 1 Cor. 14). However, the use of the written word made by our Lord in his wilderness temptation lends strong support to the view that the primary and abiding application of Paul's phrase must be to the believing use of the Scriptures as a mighty weapon in the conflict with evil. Christian experience tends to confirm this view.

(2) *The practice of prayer* (vv. 18–20).—Two words are here used for the believer's prayerful approach to God. "Prayer," the larger term, is general enough to include the whole act of worship. "Supplication," narrower in its scope, is petitionary prayer. A sharp distinction in meaning, however, is not always to be insisted upon. The use of both words here appears mainly to add intensity to the thought. The words "with all [i.e., every kind of] prayer and supplication," which in the Greek precede "praying always," are to be construed with "stand" (v. 14). Prayer is the means by which the Christian takes his stand and is the spirit or temper in which he confronts the enemy and puts him to flight.

There are times in a Christian's warfare when he feels unable to use even the sword of the Spirit as an effective weapon. Recall Bunyan's account of the experience of Christian in the Valley of the Shadow of Death. About the middle of that valley he found a place which he perceived to be "the mouth of hell." "And ever and anon," wrote Bunyan, "the flame and smoke would come out in such abundance, with sparks and hideous noises (things that cared not for Christian's sword, as did Apollyon before), that he was forced to put up his sword,

and betake himself to another weapon, called 'All-Prayer.' "
When thus he wielded this mighty weapon, the fiends of hell
"gave back and came no farther." [3] In like manner must we
also at every phase of the conflict enlist the aid of our all-
powerful God. In response to our urgent prayer he comes as a
mighty ally to stand by our side.

Paul speaks of the manner of prayer and its objects. It is
to be offered "always," literally "in every season" (v. 18). The
reference is not so much to prayer that is "without ceasing"
(1 Thess. 5:17) as it is to crisis prayer—prayer on every occasion of conflict, prayer in "the evil day." In such times of
dire need we must cry to God with special intensity. We are
to pray "in the Spirit"—under his influence and with his gracious assistance (cf. Rom. 8:26; Jude 20). And finally, such
earnest supplication requires vigilance and perseverance:
"watching . . . with all perseverance and supplication" (v.
18). "Watching" translates a word which literally means "to
keep awake" and in this context conveys the thought of never
being off guard. "Perseverance" suggests persistency, the opposite of growing weary and giving up.

For what, or for whom, are we to pray? First, and generally, we pray "for all saints" (v. 18). "No soldier entering
battle," says Hodge, "prays for himself alone, but for all his
fellow-soldiers also. They form one army, and the success of
one is the success of all." [4] The appeal is especially appropriate for our day, when so many believing people, living under
governments antagonistic to the gospel, are being viciously
assaulted by the enemy. Let us expand our vision and enlarge
our hearts so as to encompass in our prayers these and other
sorely tried Christians.

Second, and more specifically, Paul requested prayer for
himself (vv. 19–20). At two points he particularly needed
this. One was "that utterance" might "be given" to him when
he opened his mouth to speak (v. 19). Paul's hope was that
even as a prisoner he might boldly "make known the mystery

of the gospel" (v. 19). The other request also had reference to Paul's imprisonment. Remembering that for the sake of the gospel he was "an ambassador"—and this in spite of his "bonds"—he was anxious that in making known the gospel he should speak with the boldness and confidence which became his high commission from the court of heaven (v. 20).

II. THE CONCLUSION OF THE LETTER (6:21–24)

The apostle brings his majestic epistle to a close. Nothing remains to be said save a few parting words of explanation and the benediction.

1. An Explanation (vv. 21–22)

The concluding explanation concerns Tychicus and his special mission for Paul. This man the apostle highly commends as "a beloved brother and faithful minister in the Lord." (See also Acts 20:4; Col. 4:7; 2 Tim. 4:12; and Titus 3:12.) From these references we learn, among other things, that Tychicus was an Asian, a man of high character, and a trusted companion of Paul. His is the only personal name appearing in Ephesians, apart of course from those of Paul and our Lord. We may gather from the present passage that he was the bearer of this letter to its destination. In addition to this responsibility he was to give firsthand information to the recipients of the epistle concerning Paul's circumstances. In so doing, he was to comfort or encourage their hearts (vv. 21–22).

2. A Benediction (vv. 23–24)

The benediction, which actually is in two parts, gathers up several of the great words of this epistle—peace, love, faith, and grace—and expresses the apostle's fervent desire that the readers (including us) may experience with increasing fulness the reality symbolized by these words.

The final phrase of the letter, in which Paul speaks of the

recipients of grace as "them that love our Lord Jesus Christ in sincerity" (v. 24), is full of interest. Mark the breadth of it—"all them that love our Lord." In the apostle's view all who do in truth love the Lord, whatever their race, or nationality, or standing in society, are in vital contact with the grace of God, and all believing people may call them brothers. The words thus echo the emphasis on spiritual oneness that has pervaded so much of the letter.

Note the solemn fulness with which Paul speaks of the Saviour. Calling him "our Lord Jesus Christ," the apostle draws attention to the sovereignty, the humanity, and the redemptive office of our incarnate Saviour. A Christian is one who knows Jesus and loves him in all these aspects.

Finally, one must not miss the force of the last word of the epistle, translated in the King James Version by "sincerity," but more accurately rendered "incorruptibility." It is a term rich in meaning (cf. 1 Cor. 9:25; 15:52; 1 Tim. 1:17). It here characterizes the love of believers for their Lord as having an enduring, deathless quality. It is a fitting word with which to close this sublime epistle.

ACTIVITIES FOR ENRICHMENT

Consider each line of Charles Wesley's song "Soldiers of Christ, Arise" noting how the thoughts parallel those in Ephesians 6:10–20. In the song "Stand Up, Stand Up for Jesus" what words seem to be based on this passage from Ephesians?

---

[1] Alexander Maclaren, *Expositions of Holy Scripture* (Grand Rapids: Wm. B. Eerdmans Publishing Company, 1942), XVI, 338.

[2] S. D. F. Salmond, *The Expositor's Greek Testament* (Grand Rapids: Wm. B. Eerdmans Publishing Company, n.d.), III, 385.

[3] John Bunyan, *The Pilgrim's Progress* (Philadelphia: The John C. Winston Company, n.d.), p. 66.

[4] Charles Hodge, *A Commentary on the Epistle to the Ephesians* (Grand Rapids: Wm. B. Eerdmans Publishing Company, 1950), p. 392.

Suggestions for the Teacher

Who Will Lead in the Study of the Epistle to the Ephesians

SECURING INVOLVEMENT: Teacher and class members should reach an agreement as to the learning goal. Many members of your class will come with no deeper purpose than a general desire to study the Bible. Point out the purpose of the letter to the Ephesians. (See author's discussion under "The Theme of the Letter," chap. 1). Have the group read Ephesians 1:10. State that this study will show the place of the church in working out God's great purpose as stated in this verse.

Quote: "God now has a people in the world—a people in whom his purpose is being worked out and through whom he intends to effect his intention for the whole universe." Ask: What should the study of God's purpose and his plan for attaining it mean to us? Encourage responses. Challenge the group to summarize their answers in one statement of a learning goal. You may need to propose one such as the following:

LEARNING GOAL: *To seek through an exploration of the Epistle to the Ephesians to gain a sharpened awareness of God's purpose for the human race, to understand the nature and function of God's redeemed people in the world, and to recognize my place in fulfilling that function.*

FILMSTRIP: The filmstrip *Letter to Ephesus* will serve as a helpful introduction to this study, giving an overview of the entire epistle. However, you may prefer to use the filmstrip throughout the study, selecting the frames as they correlate with the respective chapters of this book.

BIBLE USING: Lead your class members to read the introduction (p. xi). Seek to have their expressed agreement as to this plan of study. Keep the emphasis on the study of the biblical text. You may wish to stay close to Dr. Vaughan's pattern as you guide your class members in Scripture study. You may vary the pattern, but your success as a teacher will consist in getting class members to let the words of the Bible itself speak to their hearts. This whole study should have a strong devotional note. As Dr. Vaughan has said, in Ephesians "Paul seems to teach on his knees." The suggested "Activities for Enrichment" at the end of each chapter emphasize this devotional character.

As each chapter is approached, begin by having the class members read the passage indicated in the heading of the chapter. After the detailed study set forth in this guidebook, again have the passage read as a whole. Point out to your class members that this procedure is basic in Bible study: Begin with the whole; study it in detail; review the whole passage again.

ACTIVITIES: Your main task as a teacher is simply to guide your members as they follow Dr. Vaughan's guidance. By way of supplement you may wish to lead them to do some of the following things. However, keep these activities supplementary; do not try to use them all; and do not let them detract from the actual study of the biblical passages.

These activities are written here as if addressed to the class members. You may wish to lead your members to examine this list and select the activities which they would like to carry out—individually or as a class.

Each member should secure for his personal use a work copy of the Bible—one which can be marked. Plan a system of Bible marking to be carried out during this entire study.

Chapter 1

1. Read the entire epistle at one sitting. You may wish to use some unfamiliar version for this reading.

2. Read Ephesians 1:10 in several versions. Discuss its significance as the key verse of the epistle. Underline the verse and print KEY VERSE in the margin of your work Bible.

3. Locate Ephesus on a map. From Acts 19; 20:17–38 learn all you can about how a church was started in that city and about Paul's concern for the work there after he left.

4. As you read, find and mark the significant "all's" in the epistle. Count the times you find this word. Discuss the significance of its frequent use.

5. Compare the salutation in Ephesians 1:1–2 with the salutations of other of Paul's epistles. Which of the epistles are addressed to saints?

6. Using a complete concordance, count the times Paul refers to himself as an apostle (1) in Ephesians and (2) in all his epistles. Discuss the significance of his frequent application of this word to himself.

Chapter 2

7. To illustrate the relationship between man's free choice and God's election, plan a poster using the idea of the inscription over the entrance to the narrow way, as referred to by Dr. Vaughan.

8. Did you decide to use a check form to depict each of the blessings discussed in this chapter? If so, did you use the following on each check: Date: *the present time;* Location: *in Christ* (or *in the heavenlies*); Payee: *the believer;* Payer: *God the Father.* In the space where the amount would be shown on a commercial check, did you show the name of a specific blessing: *redemption, forgiveness, wisdom, prudence, the Spirit.*

9. Using a red pencil, begin underlining throughout the epistle the words, phrases, and complete sentences which refer to redemption, ransom, or salvation.

10. Learn all you can about the uses of a seal in Paul's day. Consider whether each of these uses reflects some significant idea about what being sealed by the Holy Spirit means (see Eph. 1:13).

11. Find out about the payment of earnest money, both in Paul's day and now. Point out the spiritual truths implied in calling the Holy Spirit an "earnest" (see Eph. 1:14).

Chapter 3

12. As heads are bowed, have the prayer in Ephesians 1:15–23 read as the Holy Spirit's prayer for all believers. Use any favorite modern version. Seek to make this a genuine experience of being "led in prayer" by the Spirit himself.

Chapter 4

13. Begin to mark the uses of the word "walk" in this epistle. Select a color to mark all these references as you continue your study (see Eph. 2:10; 4:1,17; 5:2,8,15).

Chapter 5

14. Consider, soberly and prayerfully, the relevance of Ephesians 2:11–22 to the various racial problems in our nation.

Chapter 6

15. Trace the use of the term "mystery" in this epistle (see 1:9; 3:3,4,9; 5:32; 6:19). Select a distinguishing color and use it to underline the word "mystery" in each of these passages. In each case point out what is said to be the mystery, or secret, formerly hidden but now revealed.

16. Find, in Ephesians 3:8–9, what two great responsibilities were involved in Paul's stewardship of the mystery of the ages.

Chapter 7

17. Decide why Ephesians 4:1 is called the pivotal verse of the whole epistle. (Cf. Col. 1:10; Rom. 16:2, ASV; Phil. 1:27, ASV; 1 Thess. 2:12.)

18. In this chapter try to count the various admonitions which relate to maintaining unity in the body of Christ. As you consider a Christian's obligation to maintain unity, you will, no doubt, desire to engage in prayer about the matter.

Chapter 8

19. If a copy of *The Pilgrim's Progress* by John Bunyan is available, find the account of the experience of Christian when he came to the cross. Which items in Bunyan's account may be based on Ephesians 4:22–24? What differences are there between the aspect of the truth emphasized by Bunyan and the aspect which Paul emphasizes here? (Bunyan pictures God's act in clothing the believer with imputed righteousness; Paul urges a believer to live out this work of God in his actual daily experience.)

20. Discuss the relevance of Ephesians 5:16 as a principle to follow in witnessing; in "wayside" contacts.

Chapter 9

21. Discuss the principles which this chapter sets forth for Christian family relationships. Consider some of the difficulties faced in applying these principles. When God's standards prove difficult to apply, what course should a Christian take?

Chapter 10

22. Note the emphasis in Ephesians 6:10–20 on the believer's responsibility for putting on each piece of armor named. As the pieces are named, list them. Consider each piece, stating how a Christian should go about putting it on.

For Review and Written Work

1. What does the salutation of Paul's letter reveal about the first recipients of the epistle?

2. What does Paul say about himself in the salutation to the Ephesian epistle? Explain the significance of the statements he makes about himself.

3. What verse gives the theme of the epistle? State this theme in your own words.

CHAPTER 2

4. What is the character of a believer's blessings and what is the sphere in which they are experienced, as stated in Ephesians 1:3?

5. On what grounds do believers receive "all spiritual blessings"? What six principles are stated about God's choice in electing, or predestinating, us?

6. Name the spiritual blessings specifically mentioned in Ephesians 1:7–14.

CHAPTER 3

7. What is the main thing for which Paul gave thanks at the outset of the prayer recorded in Ephesians 1:15–23?

8. Paul prayed that the believers might possess three elements of knowledge. List these three elements, as stated in Ephesians 1:17–19.

9. What do verses 19–20 teach about the power which is available in the life of a believer? (Silently ask yourself whether you are using your available power. Do not write an answer to this comment.)

CHAPTER 4

10. Based on the description in Ephesians 2:1–3 state seven things which are true of all persons before their conversion (though not in the same degree of outward manifestation).

11. What three great experiences are set forth in Ephesians 2:4–6 relative to the Christian's position as a believer in Christ?

12. State God's twofold purpose in what he has done for believers, as set forth in Ephesians 2:7–10.

CHAPTER 5

13. Of what significance for us today is the study of the relationship between Jew and Gentile in the world of Paul's day?

14. State in your own words the five aspects of the spiritual bankruptcy which the Gentiles experienced in their unconverted state, as given in Ephesians 2:12.

15. Explain briefly the relationship of Jewish and Gentile believers in Christ, as it is set forth in Ephesians 2:13–22.

CHAPTER 6

16. Give in your own words the threefold purpose of Paul's ministry, as stated in Ephesians 3:8–13.

17. What three requests does Paul include in his prayer for believers (including us) as recorded in Ephesians 3:16–19?

18. By what means can a believer experience the answer to these requests?

CHAPTER 7

19. What is the nature of the unity which is urged upon believers as set forth in Ephesians 4? On what is it based?

20. What can Christians do to foster such unity?

21. What is the function and responsibility of each Christian in regard to the growth of the church? Explain the figure which is used in Ephesians 4:16 to set forth the idea of individual responsibility.

CHAPTER 8

22. Name some things mentioned by Paul in Ephesians 4:17–32 which a believer needs to "put off," or put out of his life.

23. In the same verses (17–32), what qualities are named that a believer should "put on" or include in his life?

24. What is the meaning of the words "redeeming the time," or "buying up the opportunity" as they relate to Christian service?

CHAPTER 9

25. Summarize the principle set forth by Paul in Ephesians 5:21–33 which should govern the relationship between a Christian husband and wife.

26. What does Ephesians 6:1–4 teach about the obligations of parents to children? Of children to parents?

27. What guidance for present-day employers and employees can be gathered from Ephesians 6:5–10?

CHAPTER 10

28. What is the sphere of a Christian's warfare? Who, or what, are his antagonists?

29. Name the pieces of armor which protect a Christian in his warfare. What is his aggressive weapon?

30. In the face of his many needs in prison, what prayer request did Paul desire to have his Ephesian friends offer for him?